Praise for Every Day is Friday: ⅃
Leaders & Entrepreneurs

"Nina captured my imagination with her title, 'Every Day is Friday.' It's really quite brilliant when you think about it. The one-day when everyone has more energy and passion because the weekend is around the corner—where we get to pursue our happiest ideals.

"Great title, but what's under the cover holds this same reflective cadence. Her personal story has always inspired me and she uses the power of storytelling in this book to weave a narrative that promotes the opportunity of self-reflection for the purpose of personal transformation. Discover yourself growing as a business leader as Nina continually surprises you with great insights on everyday business and life habits. I think you'll find her message to be both practical and attainable."

—ERIC S. YUAN, *CEO, Zoom Video Communications*

"As an entrepreneur, I was pleased to find that Every Day is Friday outlines a step-by-step action plan that I can easily implement in my own business, packed with valuable tips and information on what to expect in the coming years, to ensure I am prepared, informed and set up for success. Written from her many years of experience in business and over twenty years as a leadership coach, she shares her wisdom through not only her own personal journey, but through stories and case studies of other thriving entrepreneurs and clients to back up her claims, further proving that Nina Segura certainly knows her stuff and is truly 'walking her talk'! This book can surely help not only entrepreneurs but anyone in a leadership role in business."

—Shanda Trofe, Writing Coach & Mentor, Bestselling Author of *Authorpreneur*

"The old saying is, "Thank GOD it's Friday!" and it is all about celebrating the week's end. In Nina's beautifully crafted book, "Every Day is Friday" she gives us the simple blueprint to enjoy every day and moment of our life. Through the ACTT Blueprint for Leaders and Entrepreneurs you will learn to transition your work and life so that each day will be Friday!"

-Bill Cortright, Author of **"The New Stress Response Diet"** and **"TRUTH" The Ten-Minute Life Plan to end Procrastination**

"Nina Segura is a bright star in the Co-Active Universe. She has a great sense of what is needed in and from Leaders so that they are empowered to live their legacy in our world. If you're ready to uncover, deepen, and build on your natural strengths as a leader, read this book."

- Henry Kimsey-House, Co-Active Sage and Co-Founder of The Coaches Training Institute

Every Day is

FRIDAY

The ACTT Blueprint for Leaders and Entrepreneurs

NINA SEGURA

Foreword by J.B. Glossinger

Transcendent
Publishing

EVERY DAY IS FRIDAY

The ACTT Blueprint for Leaders and Entrepreneurs

By Nina Segura

ISBN-13: 978-0-9975209-7-2

Library of Congress Control Number: 2016948442

Author photo credit: Sharon Morgenstern Photography LLC

First Edition July 2016 Transcendent Publishing

Address:
Transcendent Publishing
PO Box 66202
St. Pete Beach, FL 33736
www.TranscendentPublishing.com

Printed in the United States of America.

DEDICATION

This book is for leaders like you who desire to live a meaningful and prosperous life no matter what changes may come. Too much fear and misunderstanding exists in our world today, primarily caused by misaligned expectations and the loss of listening deeply to ourselves for answers that truly make life worth living. This process of leaving a lasting legacy in our world starts with letting our imagination move us to our ideal future. Once we have a good idea of that, we can then make a commitment to taking one positive action step each day toward that future. In this way, we can reverse-engineer our future with our current reality. If our reality changes—as it always does—we need to make time to re-align with our **"Leader Within"** so we can do our best to deal with external situations.

Everyone has a Leader Within. This part of ourselves only wants what's best for us and those around us. We can learn to develop our connection to this part of ourselves over time. However skilled we may be at leadership, all of us will have intended and unintended impacts from the choices we make. You may be a good fit for entrepreneurship, or you may be happy working as a leader in another capacity; regardless, it's important that you are **Aligned, have a good Crew, know your Transformation Strategy and have a solid Transition Plan.**

Over the years, I've spent over a million dollars to learn how to grow a business with the highest level of integrity while leveraging the most innovative business techniques. Although I don't regret my investments, I wish there had been one place I could go, instead of the multiple avenues I had to travel, in order to quickly know what I needed to do.

After many years of experience and several mistakes, I see how important it is to enjoy work with effort and ease. There are many

Business Leaders with a prosperous AND meaningful work-life and I have humbly accepted that I am finally part of that group! I have attained this balance by committing to what really matters to me. I am not going to lie to you; I've worked hard to get where I am today.

At the same time, I will never forget the people who helped me along the way, so this book is my way of showing gratitude to those who have pointed out the markers from where I was a short while ago, to the successful path I follow today. I am now dedicated to cultivating learning experiences for myself and others so that Every Day Feels Like Friday.

By the time **you finish this book, you will have** *transformational AND practical tools you need to stay on purpose, rise above the changes that inevitably will come and have a Super Team that you can rely on to be there for you always.*

To find out more about your Leadership SuperPowers and the SuperPowers of your team visit: http://ninasegura.com/SuperPowers.

CONTENTS

FOREWORD
BY J.B. GLOSSINGER

A few years ago, I was presenting my story at a speakers' organization at a waterfront hotel in Fort Lauderdale, FL. The room was alive with so much energy, we ended the question and answer session still with many hands raised. Now, I don't do one on one coaching, my time has become more and more valuable as my business has grown. Yet, at this event, I did extend an offer for an hour of coaching to be auctioned off benefitting the speakers' organization.

The session momentum carried into the auction, and the bidding began. "Two-hundred and fifty dollars!" the emcee said, starting the bidding. A number of hands went up..." Three-hundred" ...somewhat fewer hands went up and so on. Soon, we were at seven hundred dollars with the president of the organization on my right bidding versus a determined business woman with a bright face shining at me from mid-way back on the left.

Every time the president would increase his bid, this woman, who I did not know, would beat it within a second. At almost a thousand dollars, the president, who I did know well and would have gotten tremendous value from our meeting, looked across the aisle to this unflinching woman and conceded the auction. Auction awarded to bidder name? Nina Segura.

That, my friends, was the start of my coaching and mentoring relationship with Nina. In addition to being determined, Nina is quite modest, so I'm going to say some things in this foreword that you might not hear from her. Today, Nina is a valued member of my Crew

delivering insight and value every time she engages with my Tribe. I also see her delivering that same level of insightful and intuitive intensity for her Mastermind group. Her group has transformed and found better places thanks to Nina.

Over the last twenty years, Nina has developed and integrated the tools in this book. *The ACTT Blueprint for Leaders and Entrepreneurs* has been used by spectacularly successful entrepreneurs and corporate executives to chart the next legacy-building step in their lives. Now for the first time ever, it's available to anyone who wants to take even a small action for their life's legacy by buying or borrowing this book. Standing for everyone having a life well lived is what Nina is all about, even if it means sharing tools she's spent twenty years developing for almost nothing!

Nina, simply stated, will not stop until her clients get what they intend. And what her clients intend is often times very deep work. Nina will go there with them, support them to seek their values when success in business has sidetracked them from doing what they love. "What," you might say, "How could success in business sidetrack them?"

Keep in mind her clients have all been successful, and could be successful in many different business ventures. Some started their businesses when they were very young; how many of us have made perfect decisions in our early life? Her clients have put their stake in the ground now and decided they want to have a life worth living, a legacy that does much more than pay the bills. Nina is clearly the one to walk with them and find this path. And when a leader is on this path, truly Every Day is Friday!!! I should know, I've built my business, my passion, so that I'm finished every day by 9:30am, pursuing new interests and learning the rest of the day. Does that sound like a Friday to you? Keep reading my friend.

—J.B. Glossinger

INTRODUCTION

The supreme accomplishment is to
blur the line between work and play.
-Arnold J. Toynbee

If you are trying to make sense of what is happening to you during a transition, you are not alone. The challenge with being in transition, especially when we are seasoned leaders, is to maintain the perspective that change is an opportunity for something better, and at the same time remain in touch with our feelings through the ups and downs during this period of life.

There is a specific process for making every day feel like a good and satisfied end of a hardworking week, and for some of us that feels like every day is Friday!!! **The ACTT Blueprint for Leaders and Entrepreneurs** provides practical business tools and the mindset necessary *for your next success, whether that is having a more fulfilling work-life or transitioning away from your current position altogether! So whether you're looking for stronger leadership skills or are in career transition, you might:*

- Feel frozen in pursuit of your life's work or your legacy as a leader.

- Have trouble relating to your co-workers or your family about your dreams.

- Be afraid that your work-life is putting a strain on your relationships and money.

- Need to refocus on your purpose as a Leader so you can take your work-life to the next level and beyond.

iii

The real problem might be:

- You have a high workload and an abundance of family priorities AND aren't sure how to have the freedom and flexibility you want without risking your financial security.

- You are hesitant or just don't want to talk to people at work about your plans for fear of feeling exposed.

- You want something better and you don't want to lose the good you have in your life.

- You are tired of doing work and life alone.

You know it and I know it, when we are fulfilled at work we are happier at home, and when we are happier at home the world is a better place. *The ACTT Blueprint for Leaders and Entrepreneurs* is a simple but not always easy blueprint for your work-life.

Although I am known as a practical transformation expert, I recognize that I can't create transformation on my own. Part of my journey has always involved the right people being around me to support my continuing growth and development. With your commitment to applying what you learn in this book, your journey will be a life-changing experience. Take a moment and explore the possibilities with me. I invite you to keep reading and take from this book what works best for you.

Why You Should Read this Book!

Okay truth be told I hate the word should but I wanted to get your attention. You know it's time to read this book when you are ready to do something—anything—different. You may or may not check all the boxes by answering all of my questions and that is okay. I just know that whatever you do must be better than doing nothing. This book is like anything else—what you put into it you'll get out of it.

> *Personally, I'm always ready to learn,*
> *although I do not always like being taught.*
> *-Winston Churchill*

CHAPTER ONE
ONCE UPON A TIME

Before we get started, let me tell you a little about who I am. I am a real person just like you; filled with strengths and scars trying to make the world a better place. Although I am a tenacious life-long learner, things haven't always been easy. For a variety of reasons, which you will discover as you read this book, I married for the first time at age of 43 to a man who was truly worth waiting for. I have two step-daughters, and most of the time we like each other! I am the founder of Metaspire Consulting (MetaspireConsulting.com), and creator of BusinessCoachingOnDemand.com and SuperVirtualTeams.com. I am a practical transformation expert, leadership coach, experiential speaker and thanks to you a published author!

I am guessing you're a lifelong learner too because you are reading this book. But before we get further acquainted, I want you to know my hope is that as you continue to read this book you will feel inspired to take positive steps toward living your life more fully and in harmony with who you really are and what you really want to achieve.

My life is so good today. I am very grateful for all of the coaches, therapists, "adopted" family and mastermind leaders who made me who I am today. Without that work, my husband and I wouldn't be happily married nor would I love my clients and my work. However, things weren't always that way. I used to think that only people who were born with money could make money. I used to think maybe I did something bad in a previous life so I couldn't be successful.

In fact, one of my earliest memories is unsuccessfully trying to stop my father from hitting my sister. She ran upstairs. He chased her. I screamed for my mom to stop it. She said, "If you want him to stop, you tell him." I ran up the stairs screaming, "Stop!" like a broken record. When he finished hitting her, I offered her my teddy bear. She refused. As tears ran down our cheeks, my chest felt frozen. I didn't know what I was feeling but it wasn't good.

Now I know it was my first experience with the feeling of helplessness. This early experience taught me something: My parents' way of communicating as life-partners and raising children would not work for me. I felt a power within myself rising up which said, "There must be something better than this." **This "Voice" is what I call the Leader Within, God or our Intuition. Some call it our Captain, our Pilot, or our Higher Self. Whatever you call it, this is a part of us we are born with and our connection can develop over time.**

On the other hand, I learned from that experience, when I was younger, not to bother asking for help because if you want something done, you have to do it yourself. My parents talked to me like I was an adult, which led to a boat-load of issues for me (like feeling pressure to know the answer before any questions were asked). Although for years I argued that clearly the stork dropped me in the wrong house, the gift here became my strong value of self-reliance.

Something else was created from that frightening event. When my sister, who was nine years older than me at the time, refused the teddy bear I had offered her, I took it as a personal rejection and the "cancerous belief" that "I am not enough" made its deep scar in my young psyche. The truth is, I still struggle with this limiting belief even now. In fact, I know that when my jaw begins to clench, I need to take a serious step back. *If you struggle with perfectionism, what is the value you are trying to live out?* For me, it was that I wanted to feel valuable. Think back over your own past experiences that may have created subconscious influencers which have bubbled to the surface over the years. Later in this book you'll have a spot to take some notes.

It was early spring of 1976, and I was about seven years old. It's a cool, crisp ordinary day and my parents' arguing is getting louder. I look down and notice my brother's football uniform lying on the carpet. I reach down and pick up the helmet and try to pull it on. This padding is comfy even though it's slipping a bit. My parents' voices are dimmer. It's PERFECT!

I imagine I could wear it every day and it would protect me from random acts of family violence. I didn't want to take the helmet off. I am not sure why my mom had such a hard time understanding that. I still think that was a good idea. ***Anyway, the point here is that as children we are automatically aligned with our values of imagination and resourcefulness***. So it's important to get back to that natural state. **Having our imagination and resourcefulness intact are huge benefits to us when we are in transition, have big decisions to make or are goal setting.** Now it's your turn.

Memories

1. What's one of the first impacting memories you have?

2. What did you believe about yourself at that time? What did you believe about the world around you?

3. What do you believe now? How strongly do you believe it?

4. What are you willing to do or not do based on the belief of your choosing?

At age eleven, I, with my mom and my sister closest in age, moved from upstate New York to Hollywood, Florida with no financial support from my father. I grew up in a relatively poor rural area. When I started high school, we upgraded to a single-wide trailer with no air conditioning. If you know the word "confederate," you would under-stand the trailer park where we lived in Davie, Florida. Cars up on blocks in the front yard, rebel flags galore. So, it was interesting being a poor Spanish, Jewish girl from New York living in Davie, of course I lost that NY accent real fast.

As I look back on those times, I had no idea who I was nor what it felt like to feel fully alive—yet something inside me was beating within my heart. When I asked my oldest sister, Barbara, about my hopeless feelings, she told me about this thing called God. She explained that God was bigger than all of us humans and loved us unconditionally.

Although I couldn't reconcile being a by-product of a misguided stork, I felt a warmness in my heart.

As a kid, I would often hold my breath just to hear my heartbeat. I knew everyone alive had a heartbeat and as I got older I realized that I didn't start my heart and I couldn't stop my heart either. This inspired me to know for sure that there is a higher purpose for me and everyone.

We live in a diverse world, but the fact that our hearts are beating is one truth that connects us. I invite you now to put your hand where you can feel your heartbeat. Take a deep breath and consider that **maybe God gave us our heartbeat to remind us of the kind, steady force of love that exists inside of us and to remind us of our true nature— being lovable and alive**. Although at the time, I continued to believe that surviving was what life was about. I stayed inside and sang a lot. **"*In the summertime mom and I would sing, she'd tell me about the dreams of my family and all the things she wanted for me. She sang to me as the day went by, I wanna live, not only survive.*" My mom was a professional singer and although she never really sang those italicized words above, I wished she had.

The Corporate Life

One day, I had enough of being my mother's emotional support system. So I aligned myself with my sense of adventure and left the single-wide trailer at seventeen. I focused on getting a "secure" job because I just wanted to feel safe when I walked home at night. I thought I was really "living" when I landed the customer service position at American Express (Amex). Now I had more than a job. I had a CAREER at Amex. Who would believe that a girl who came from a trailer park in Davie, Florida would have the opportunity to work her way up the corporate ladder?

At the time, I sang at Calvary Chapel, Fort Lauderdale, and an opportunity came up to serve in Moscow. Given my sense of adventure, I quit my job and moved to Russia for a few months. The day I got back from Moscow, my car engine died. For a number of reasons, the church no longer continued to be a place in which I wanted to be of service. I worked with a band and wrote a few albums. It was an incredibly fulfilling time in my life but that wasn't getting me a meaningful and prosperous life of my dreams anytime soon. So I called my previous boss from Amex and asked for my job back; luckily I got it.

Fast-forward 17 years; the customer service girl became a global reengineering project manager in WW Technologies, restructuring international operations in Amex. I was saving the company millions of dollars on multi-year projects. All the time I was accomplishing that, I was so into the career track that I managed to earn a Master's degree in Business at night and became an expert (Black Belt) in Six Sigma. My team and I even won the prestigious Chairman's Award for Quality. The leadership and business experience I received from American Express is unparalleled. I should have been very pleased with myself, right?

Yet, something was still missing. I'd done everything THEY wanted me to do and more, I had made millions of dollars for THEM, but **I wasn't living the life I had imagined for myself**—whatever that was! That small voice (Leader Within) was gnawing at my consciousness again, sending me the uncomfortable message that something was amiss, and it needed to change. Was it telling me to lower my expectations and career aspirations, or to dig deeper into why I had that empty feeling?

I decided to dig deeper. Seventeen years working my way up the corporate ladder and do you know what arriving at a long-term goal felt like? For me, I felt completely numb. Perhaps the "top" was just someone else's definition of the top and not mine? That thought led me to the larger query: was the life I was leading not really my ideal life, the one that reflected who I really was? Was I aligning myself with somebody else's illusion for what was right for me? This was not the feeling of security my mom wanted me to have when she celebrated my job at American Express. Indeed, that empty feeling started the internal debate usually referred to as the "Mid-life Crisis."

I had great relationships at work, but my heart broke for a few of the women I admired who started acting like men—denying their feelings, not being appropriately vulnerable in conversations, and even sometimes losing their hair. I knew something was missing. I began to question what I wanted out of the future. Suddenly, the mental structure that supported my vision for the future was melting away; I felt lost and disoriented. Then an "invitation" arrived.

It was a letter from my CIO "inviting" me to look for another position at Amex, or take an envelope full of severance. I am sure that I was the only one on my team imagining myself doing cartwheels down the cubicle aisle when I heard this news. I was satisfied because I went as far as I wanted to go with my career at Amex. Truth be told, I really did seriously think about doing these cartwheels down the aisle. I even practiced one at home just to make sure I could pull it off. I mean, what would they do about it? Fire me?

I didn't know what I was going to do for work but I knew that there was something better for me than reapplying for a different job within Amex. So I did what every reasonable person would do. I took a few mental health days and drove down to the Florida Keys, composing yet another song: **"*I was staring at the inbox. They didn't pay me enough. With stress every day; it wasn't worth the 401k. I had to make a way. Not drive 45 minutes every day; find a better quality of life. Not a sacrifice. Can you believe I am talking barefoot sitting here? Now I go where the street takes me. Down in the Keys where the sunlight dances through the trees.*" And just like that, those practical benefits lost their motivating power over me. I needed a better quality of life and not just more sacrifice for some *potential* retirement check in the uncertain future.

My department was being dismantled and I was at a crossroads. I had left Amex before to be a missionary and to do some singing gigs but I always came back to my home at Amex. Memories, relationships and the warmth I'd felt there faded away. I imagine it was emotionally similar to a divorce without kids.

When it rains, well, I hope that it's just rain. Coming from Florida, I am no stranger to hurricanes. In the middle of my contemplations and severance from Amex, my brother who is 11 years older than I called me and said he had been diagnosed with cancer from a contaminated water supply in Camp Lejeune. Which added another "holy s%^#" moment and anxiety to follow, with questions about the future. I wasn't sure what I was going to do but being a "deer in the headlights" was not me. Indeed, the "invitation" from my CIO became just the incentive I needed to take action and gain control of my life.

At that time, I didn't understand what that really meant or how I was going to make it happen, but I decided I was going to switch from the reactive, victimized, insecure employee and become proactive in my pursuit of who I really wanted to be and how I would make it happen. Against any obvious reasoning, I was one of the only people actually happy about my department being dismantled. My inner teenager helped me write this song: **"*You say I am crazy and you don't want to listen, you got an answer for everything. Get out now. Out of my way. Get out now."* American Express made me in large part the leader I am today. I have no ill will towards that company, and yet it was time to move on!

So, humor me when I pose my next questions to you. Relax, give me a chance. **Ask yourself what makes you feel fully alive? What do you love so much that you lose track of time? Does just the thought of that awaken something inside you?** We are talking about the F-word here. Depending on your mindset, it may not mean what you think it means.

Within the context of this book, the "F-word" stands for "feelings." I find that much unhappiness stems from a misplaced focus on our careers or money problems. In my experience, too many Business Leaders find that they are not in alignment with their thoughts AND feelings. During the first part of our lives we typically strive for the false sense of security that money brings. The role we play at work or at home becomes enmeshed with that drive for financial stability and takes over any feelings of enjoyment or satisfaction for our accomplishments.

In particular, men aren't prone to measure their success with the way they feel. They are conditioned to buy into the "brave hunter out there providing for the family." When men are in touch with their thoughts AND feelings, they know what true success is all about. My hope is that my generation will be the last to get money and feeling successful confused. People won't remember what shirt we wore, but they will remember how they felt around us. How much time do we spend thinking about what we wear, and for what? Of course, I know we need to look good to feel good but most of us can do with a little less self-indulgence and more internal alignment. **When we feel successful we are successful no matter how much money is in the bank. Money does give us choices. However, as we get older the need for financial achievement is lessened and the desire for significance is greater. Our ego-driven typical work-life decisions just no longer work for us.**

**To hear Nina's Original Songs, "I Wanna Live," voice "Down in the Keys" and "Get Out Now" visit: http://ninasegura.com/

Values

It's commonly understood that value is what I get for my money. However, as a management consultant, I wrote business cases to save hundreds of thousands – often millions of dollars. **I remember being with a client one day who seemed resistant to the savings value I calculated. So I looked at her and said, "Look, you're going to save almost 100 million dollars. What's the problem?" I won't go there now, but what I realized is that savings on paper is not savings in reality when the culture is not ready for it. Now I know what really runs a company are the values of its people.**

Of course we're in business to make money, but in Six Sigma I learned that when we focus on value, the money follows. The problem is that most Business Leaders don't know what their personal values are, nor do they know how to listen for integral values. **Successful Business Leaders, like the client I mentioned above, know that personal values are NOT an outlier to be removed from a process.** I now strongly believe that; **how much we honor our values impacts our energy and ultimately our life purpose.**

Although personal values are a rarely spoken language in our culture, they are our internal compass for how we think the world should work. We all have values in common, but what we're looking for here are your personal core values that are as unique to you as your fingerprints. For those of you that are unsure of your values, I completely get it. It's not dinner conversation, and we don't learn about it in high school, yet they impact us every day. Although a good coach will support you in understanding your own unique values, we are going to do an exercise to get you aligned with some of your personal values. In this way, you will be more aligned with who you really are.

My experience when working with fulfilled Business Leaders shows that they have an alignment of personal values with their business goals. Indeed, these are not mutually exclusive! In fact, my methodology as a practical transformation expert starts with a deep dive into aligning the personal values of the Business Leader before tackling the more conventional and well-known solutions to running a business.

Personal Values

Many leaders never start on some things they know they need to do because they fear that they can't have what they want AND meet their business goals. It's IMPORTANT to know your values BEFORE planning your goals because personal values are the undercurrent of what impacts our choices (how we spend our time, how we spend our money).

Sample Values Sheet

On the following page, circle five values for which you have the most resonance (feel free to add your own):

Accomplishment	Achievement	Acknowledgement	Adventure	Aesthetics
Ambition	Authenticity	Balance	Beauty	Being of Service
Belonging	Calmness	Carefulness	Collaboration	Commitment
Community	Compassion	Competitiveness	Connection	Consistency
Contentment	Contribution	Cooperation	Courageousness	Courteous
Creativity	Curiosity	Decisiveness	Dependability	Determination
Diligence	Directness	Discipline	Discretion	Diversity
Effectiveness	Efficiency	Elegance	Empathy	Empowerment
Enjoyment	Enthusiasm	Environment	Equality	Excellence
Excitement	Expertise	Exploration	Expressiveness	Fairness
Faith	Family	Fidelity	Fitness	Flexibility
Fortitude	Freedom	Friendship	Fun	Generosity
Grace	Growth	Happiness	Hard work	Harmony
Health	Honesty	Honor	Humility	Humor
Imagination	Independence	Ingenuity	Integration	Insightfulness
Integrity	Joy	Justice	Learning	Legacy
Love	Loyalty	Mastery	Merit	Nurturing
Obedience	Openness	Order	Originality	Participation
Patriotism	Peace	Philanthropy	Playfulness	Positivity
Practicality	Preparedness	Productivity	Professionalism	Prudence
Quality Time	Quality	Recognition	Reliability	Resilience
Resourcefulness	Results	Risk Taking	Romance	Security
Self-care	Self-control	Self-development	Self-reliance	Sensitivity
Serenity	Shrewdness	Simplicity	Spirituality	Spontaneity
Stability	Strength	Structure	Success	Teamwork
Temperance	Thankfulness	Thoroughness	Thoughtfulness	Thriftiness
Timeliness	Tolerance	Tradition	Trust	Uniqueness

Self-Reflection Values Exercise

How did it go circling only five values? Was it easy to do or did you find yourself wanting more than five values? You see, when we were kids we had no problem blurting out, "I wanna be a doctor, or a ballerina." As kids we would just *naturally* dive in and express our values. What happens as we get older though is we are often tempted to be too much of an adult, have too many adult-like goals AND when we don't tap into our inner child's ambitions and honor those values, we are apt to behave like an angry teenager.

The angry teenager is more likely to make unconscious and misdirected decisions. You see it every day, people looking for a geographical cure, or buying expensive things they don't need, another tattoo, a few more units of Botox, or worse yet, destroying good relationships by being addicted to something. Remember a moment ago when I asked you about your values? Now we're going to use that information.

1. Today my top five values are:

    a. _____

    b. _____

    c. _____

    d. _____

    e. _____

2. On a scale from 1-10 (10 being the most), how fully are you living your set of values today?

    a. _____

    b. _____

    c. _____

    d. _____

    e. _____

3. Values are something we are born with and evolve over time. Keeping in mind the five values you've just identified, think back to when you were younger and answer the following questions. Note: You may have more than one career for each question. Try to just pick one at a time; the key is to understand your innate values so that you can express them more fully, regardless of your current career.

   - When I was a kid I wanted to be a/an_____ when I grew up.

   - When I was a teenager I wanted to be a/an_____ when I grew up.

   - When I was a young adult I wanted to be a/an _____ _____.

4. Based on the previous answers, how does what you wanted to be, inform you today about what is still important to you? _____.

5. The one value you would most like to honor today is _____.

6. What would life be like if you were to honor that value more fully? _____ _____.

7. How would honoring this value make a difference in your yearly goals? _____.

When we are in transition, making a decision or setting goals, we will typically hear a few different voices in our head. As we get older, and continue to evolve, we need to manage those parts of ourselves that get to make the final decision. If you want every day to be like a Friday for yourself, then you need to tap into that child-like imagination of yours. After that, bring in your healthy teenager, you know, the one that likes to challenge the status quo? You'll need this sense of adventure to motivate you to do something different.

In transition we are going to fail. We are going to have to get back up. So the healthy parent inside of us must also be heard to help us with self-compassion and good boundaries. Having the consciousness to understand what is happening in our own minds is the mindset we need to maintain positive forward-focused movement. **Like I said earlier, when we do this work, a trusted coach or mentor can help us identify our personal values because sometimes others who know us see the way we respond to life's situations in ways that we can often forget.**

Change is constant and seemingly accelerating. Convoluted and increasingly esoteric economics and globalization are playing an increasingly important role in modern life—some might say too important. There is a lot of fear and unhappiness out there, even for those of us who have met the definition of "being successful." So, open your mind and be prepared to challenge yourself and the "F-word," your feelings. Think about how you want to feel when you reach the end of this book. You will be all the better for it.

Beauty for Ashes

As my brother began his road back to healing, I headed straight to work with a coach. I decided that although I was afraid, I wanted my own business. I wasn't sure I had the stomach for the ups and downs that all Business Owners go through, but I was going to do it even if I had to run through my 401k money. Career coaches didn't help you open a business at that time like we do at BusinessCoaching-OnDemand.com. And yet, as I look back, that desire to start my own business had been always knocking around somewhere in my subconscious. It was just the fear of failure and financial insecurity (no more trailers for me!) that had kept it buried. I remembered what Joseph Campbell, the great mythologist, had said, and I repeated it to myself over and over:

If you follow your bliss, you put yourself on a kind of track that has been there all the while, waiting for you, and

the life that you ought to be living is the one you are living. Wherever you are—if you are following your bliss, you are enjoying that refreshment, that life within you, all the time.
-Joseph Campbell

Philosophy is important but so is reality. After the post-partum from the Amex relationship, money was running short and I cried out to God one day, saying, "I am not taking any more money from my 401k. I will continue to follow my bliss even if I have to sell luggage door to door before I have a successful business. Oh, and I hope you don't ask me to do that." Unbearable silence followed and I erupted inside. So I asked for what I wanted, "I want a job working from home making $125.00 an hour, and I want to work in world-wide marketing." A little voice in my head said, "Yeah right. Like that's going to happen." (That was not my Leader Within talking.) To which I replied, "I am asking for it anyway." The next day came and went. There was no answer. The time for introspection and discontent gave way to a sudden burst of energy directing me to take action.

I called all my friends in my industry who knew what I could do and let them know I was looking for work. Two weeks later, I got a call to do a three-week consulting contract as a process analyst. Six years after, that initial three-week consulting contract had me working as a process architect for Hewlett-Packard WW Marketing & Indirect Sales. We worked together to facilitate world-wide process changes that saved HP $67 million within the first year! There it was; a way to leverage my skills, knowledge and experience within my own business!

Millions of Dollars, Baby

In 2005, I formalized my business and founded Metaspire LLC., the **first certified woman-owned holistic management consulting company in South Florida.** My years of working for a Fortune 100 company were transformed into a personal asset. My life was suddenly occupied with problem solving for dream clients like of Land O'Lakes, Inc. JPMorgan Chase, BCBS Excellus and of course, HP, which started it all.

I put my own Super Virtual Team together, and we did many projects that saved clients millions of dollars. It was an amazing experience to be personally responsible for helping those companies achieve their goals and make life easier for their employees. That was also when I made millions of dollars in revenue within the first five years! Imagine, this amazing company. I have an amazing team and PROFITS. I have all the luxuries I want; surely every day was Friday for me, right? NOT!

I thought to myself, "I have all the luxuries I want. Why do I feel like something is still missing?" That damned small intuitive voice was pestering me again. What now! Was it a form of "I want-it-all," or was I missing something at the edge of my consciousness?

What Could Possibly Be Wrong?

Further introspection revealed:

- I had founded a wildly successful company and was still feeling unfulfilled.

- I saved millions of dollars for other companies, a job that I loved doing, but I felt like I still wasn't making a difference in people's lives.

- I had walked away from the values, creativity, and intuition that had kept me going in my life.

One night I woke up crying. I dreamt that my mom was going to pass away. Someone in my dream had asked me if there was anything else I needed to say to her and I replied, "No." But nothing could prepare me for the serendipitous shock that happened next.

Our Mother Has Died

The year was 2010, on a crystal-clear, and soon-to-be-agonizing, Florida evening, when I got a call from my sister and brother saying,

"Our mother has died." My first thought was: eighty years of survival, and very little of the life she had wanted. A severely overweight and sedentary woman, she passed away alone when her heart gave out. A few days later, my siblings and I arrived at her apartment, trash bags in hand, to dispose of the stale Cheetos and roach bait under the couch cushions.

As we emptied the pantry, we joked about who could find the oldest expiration date on the bottom of the cans. Yes, we found such old useless things, but we also found delicate hand-colored photos of my mom when she was a torch singer in New York City and passionately sang with my father. This once-beautiful woman with a sultry singing voice who could charm the sun to rise early, passed with her songs stuck in her heart, leaving barely a trace of the impact she wanted to make on this world.

As those thoughts passed through my mind, I suddenly had a breakthrough moment. A voice deep inside me spoke again, "If I were to die now, what would my life have meant?" Okay, I had planned to leave all my money to my family and charity, but was that all that would be left to mark my presence on this earth? I thought to myself, "I have money but I am so lonely." I know it's easier to do "things" than to care about people. People can be very complex and too often interpersonal relationships are complicated. Then I thought, "How would people define me if I should pass away today?" I imagined they would say, "That Nina, she was the most profitable international restructuring expert I have ever known." Or, "That Nina, she was such a hard worker."

There I was, with all the outward trappings of success—and I still felt lonely, unfulfilled, and without a meaningful legacy to contribute to this world. I didn't put my health first, didn't put relationships first, and was a lone ranger without a "Crew." I had success by most standard definitions, yet success seemed empty and without much real meaning other than having given me a decent financial statement.

Somehow, I knew these feelings weren't held by only me. With the modern lifestyle and changing values, the focus on consumption and competition may be crippling, and distracting from certain basic human needs. As I walked my dogs in the park one day, I realized maybe those distractions were guiding me to another career or whatever it was that I was missing.

Doing Something Different

A few months after that epiphany, I got a call from a former client inviting me to lunch later that week. From the first day I met him, I knew there was something special and familiar about him. However, for a variety of reasons, we kept our relationship strictly business. As we sat down outside by the Intracoastal for lunch at the Blue Moon Fish Company in Fort Lauderdale, I could tell he liked me and I was ready to do what I always did with good guys like him. Run! As soon as lunch was over I thanked him and rushed outside for the valet to get my car. Yet inside I was wanting to stay with him. As we both waited for our cars, he leaned over and asked me for a date. My mind said, "No!" and my mouth said "Yes!" I was like, 'Mouth, you betray me!' I immediately called my mentor, Lillian, and asked her for advice. She said, "Nina, you will never know what this guy is like if you don't give him a chance."

A few weeks later, our first date was to visit an art show in Delray Beach, and we've been inseparable ever since. My husband Jeff and I married under a Tiki hut in Delray Beach. My two step-daughters, Mariel and Ayden, were a very special part of our ceremony. The point is sometimes we are looking so closely for an answer in one area of our life that we often miss something of far more significance in another.

How is Your Day Going?

- Take an inventory of your day today, how many hours were you on autopilot?
- On an average day, how much time do you spend taking care of the following:

Your health? Significant other? Friends? Family? Your career? Your finances? Your living environment? Work environment? Your relationships? Personal or professional growth? Your legacy as a leader? How much time do you really want to be spending on each of those?

The Labyrinth

A few years after Jeff and I married, I committed to Coach and Leadership Training at The Coaches Training Institute (CTI). During one of the Leadership retreats in California, I walked through a laid-out labyrinth. If you've walked a labyrinth before, you know that the process is to focus only on the one step ahead of you. In this way, you can't see the end of where you are going or where you've been. I was disoriented; the Theseus and Minotaur thing.

Well, it certainly felt that way. Towards the center of it, I felt this warm feeling, like a soft blanket of love wrapped around me, as an epiphany came of knowing that my role is to point people to their centers; to their own Leader Within who will guide them through the labyrinth of life. The physical metaphor became obvious. Indeed, I believe everyone is born with this gut feeling or intuition...the small voice whispering to them, reminding them of their purpose. However, the complex, exciting and intriguing world around us makes it hard for most of us to hear our Leader Within. Fortunately, locating that small voice is something we can learn and develop over time.

I realized during the retreat that although I was expressing one of my highest values, freedom of full self-expression as a Business Owner, I *wasn't making a difference in people's lives. You know what it feels like when we're not making a difference in people's lives? That's right,* it feels *useless.* **I had to fire that part of myself that said "work-schedule flexibility at all costs" because it no longer outweighed the value of wanting to be of service.** So at this time, after some inner reflection and many conversations with Jeff, I had to exercise some self-compassion for getting caught up in the *things* of this world, not the *people* in this world.

Since that realization at the labyrinth, I have committed myself to work with people who I respect and enjoy; people who are committed to seeking their own fulfillment, even if they aren't happy all the time. Truly, I chose to make my work and life more meaningful for me. I chose to help people identify and live their dream. In theory, it all sounded good, but how was I going to actually accomplish that goal? Although my life experiences have been better from all of my training as a Co-Active Coach and Leader, they missed teaching me about another very important "F-word," FINANCES!

Benevolent Ignorance

I made up my mind that I was ONLY going to help people through coaching. All of us have something to give, and I have a talent for metaphors and asking powerful questions, especially within the business context. I had enough years and experience to understand the conflicts, external and internal, that keep many of us, including myself, from having a "life well-lived." So, I took the following actions:

- I walked away from the financial security of global re-engineering projects and high-profile clients.

- I quickly shifted my focus to coaching and spent my time at the Chamber of Commerce, trying to develop contacts and potential coaching clients, but that turned out to be a total bust; nobody was buying and everyone was selling, just like me! I volunteered like crazy for The Society for Organizational Learning (Peter Senge's Organization) and other coaching organizations. I realized that I was NOT the outlier, the special provider. It turned out to be a huge mistake spending all my time in my own community with people who saw no real use or value to the skills I was offering them.

- Then I invested heavily in technology. I created LinkedIn and Google ads and keywords. At the time, if you looked up "Executive Coach Fort Lauderdale" I was first in Google search results! Hooray! So, where were all the clients? Only about four people per year search for that term. On top of that, it costs hundreds of thousands of dollars to stay at the top of the first page of a Google search.

Later, I realized that I invested in volunteering and technology as a way to hide. I wanted someone or something else to solve the puzzle of why my marketing and sales processes weren't working. And at the same time as I finished CTI's Leadership program, which added quality and meaning to my personal and professional life, I realized most consulting focuses only on the mechanics of identifying business problems and solutions.

My value now as a coach and consultant goes far beyond just fixing business problems. Coaching is about a thought provoking conversation and letting our hearts and imaginations move us toward a better outcome for ourselves and the community around us; which is particularly important for conscious Business Leaders.

As a lone ranger most of my life, I hesitated to be close to my community. However, as I studied Napoleon Hill, Dale Carnegie, Richard Branson, and Robert Kiyosaki, I discovered that fulfilled AND financially successful people have a few powerful things in common, which I practice now and will discuss in detail in the chapter three.

Today

Most days, my husband and I have a healthy breakfast together and sit outside by our pool. We talk about our plans that day and design how we will "be" with one another. He goes off to work and my heart leaps as I head joyfully to my home office. I run several practical transformational leadership programs that include one-on-one co-aching, masterminds and all the career, business and leadership tools our clients need. We're committed to customizing solutions for our clients. So that means we only take about 20-30% of the clients that wish to work with us.

I am finished with work typically by 3pm every day with the exception of when my Crew needs me. My husband and I enjoy biking on nature trails, walking through Butterfly World (well, me more than him on that one) and supporting local artists. We have a great life together, and I wouldn't have any of this if I didn't take chances AND responsibility for what I was wanting.

We are both aligned on our highest values. Today, when my values feel conflicted, I call on my Crew, which I will talk about later in this book. I am no longer misaligned, no longer alone, no longer without a plan. Having my Leader Within as the captain of my ship, I align all parts of myself. Not perfectly. Of course not. However, I honor my childlike imagination and tap into the adventure of my inner teenager. When I fail, which I have now given myself permission to do up to 10,000 times a day, I tap into the unconditional love of a parent, and have become an adult, knowing when to tap into each part of me. Now that makes Every Day a Friday. But enough about me.

What's Your Story?

1. Now that you've heard my story, what is your story?

2. How will you let yourself be more curious and imaginative?

3. What is the most adventurous thing you've ever done? How can that energy help you with your next big success?

4. How will you develop your connection with your Leader Within?

If you've taken time to answer the above questions, congratulations! Most of us become what other people want us to be. It's just the way we are conditioned from childhood. Our culture, parents, peers, spouse, and employers have influence over who we think we should be, which may not be who we really are. When we take time to fully explore who we are and let our feelings run their course, we find ourselves off a hamster wheel that doesn't belong to us or serve us.

CHAPTER TWO
THIS AIN'T NO DISCO

Nothing is more constant than
change -Heraclitus (535 B.C.)

It's not climate change, terrorism or financial uncertainty that continues to cast a shadow on our times. Something deeper and more personal is happening. In the United States, the engine of world growth, change, opportunity and the keeper of individualism and human potential—we can feel those gathering winds of change coming towards us. Some of us fear the worst. Others trust that those winds will fill their sails and take them to new horizons. Which perspective do you have?

Many of my clients initially feel like everything they've worked and sacrificed for is just not enough, or that their dream is slipping away. Others are confused about what their dream is at this point in their life. We now have an opportunity to ask ourselves if we are doing what "they" expect of us or what we expect of ourselves. Being passionate about your job is not some sort of "pie-in-the-sky" idealistic chatter. Do you think you can do what you love and not work a day in your life?

Shift Happens

- What in your professional life is waiting to shift for the better?
- On a scale from 1 to 10 (ten being the most), how successful do you feel right now (notice I didn't say how much money is in the bank)?

- On a scale from 1 to 10, how willing are you to align your actions with your goals? (It all starts with willingness!)

- How successful do you want to feel after reading this book?

The Socio-Economic Backdrop

After World War II, the USA was the only real economy left standing with the ability to expand its domestic and international markets. It was a fertile time for the concept of capitalism and combined with the technologies spawned from the War, the economy and society of the USA started an exponential economic expansion for over half a century. It lifted an entire society off the farm and into cars that transported them to their new "micro tribe"—the work place. As the magic potion of consumption and new economics began to take center stage in modern society, insidious developments started to occur—like when we began thinking that our work was our community.

Families started splitting up as newly educated children began to pursue new and exciting careers. Wherever those jobs demanded their total commitment, they moved. Soon, the job and career became the provider of all things: wealth, prestige, friends, class distinction, and...to many, the reason for living. Those folks chose—and are still choosing—to *"Live to work, not work to live."* No longer was it important what your parents did or what their last names were. Workers and professionals became classified by what they did for a living. *Workers and professionals alike became members of a national tribe according to what they provided to the economy and not so much what they provided to themselves and the community around them.* Life became centered on the job and the distractions and complexities of the wealth and consumption that job would bring.

Producing items for consumption became the foundation and driving force that made the United States great, economically speaking. Few (except children—especially teenagers) asked the question: *"What happens when everybody has everything they need?"* The home, the car, the vacation, the future security of a pension and retirement plan. The distinction between wants and needs became clouded. What motivated people to keep going to work every day when they had it all? The simple answer is that consumption became an unspoken addiction to many.

The need to keep consumption going gave birth to new techniques in marketing that refined the appetite for more of the "essential needs" that drives the consumer society. Seventy percent of the USA GDP is consumer based. When you stop to think about it, it's truly an amazing concept: Creating and fulfilling the needs of others can provide not only our survival and comfort but also construct a framework on which to build our lives.

Meanwhile, the rest of the world looked on, its eyes on the United States. Some of the world watched with envy and others disdain as the material standard of living increased for most Americans. It continued on a long and steady climb to home ownership, multiple cars in the driveway, university educations, second homes, boats, vacations, and other cool goodies. Further along with that amazing trend came the dark side of leveraged consumption and overpowering materialism.

Between the late 1960s and 1990s the dynamics of population growth, supply and demand, the incredible growth of the large multinational-industrial companies and the growing focus on short-term growth over long-range planning put into play a series of subtle factors that have been eroding the base of what U.S. citizens used to accept as inevitable entitlements: growth, security and a meaningful life; the American Dream.

Debt and overextension of credit—the life blood for economic growth—created tremendous stress on those borrowers who found themselves at the wrong place, or made bad decisions at the wrong time in the business cycle. Losing a job could trigger the almost complete destruction of not only a person's assets like autos and homes and future access to credit, but also precipitate divorce and the loss of self-image and confidence in the dream.

With the passing of Y2K (remember the extremists warning us to not get stuck in the elevator at midnight on December 31st, 1999?), American life started to change. No longer did a good education automatically transition into a good job with a stable company. For the most part, gone were the days of the lifetime relationship of working for the same company. Long gone were the days of loyalty to each other and "the company." Divorce rates held steady. Church attendance declined as science, technology and home-based spirituality began providing faster results.

The average employee continues to change jobs about every eighteen months and professionals can expect to have multiple careers over their lifetimes. However, this is not the kind of change Heraclitus was talking about in 535 B.C.! There are no guarantees, with the exception of change.

Change is Nature's Tool and Evolution is its Goal

Physicists and cosmologists will tell you that chaos and entropy are the very fabric of the physical universe. As conscious human beings, we are challenged by our intelligence to evolve; to help solve the never-ending problems that come our way—both environmental and self-created. It's the way of nature, or as some would say: God, The Source, or our Higher Power's way of helping us develop ourselves. When we believe things can work <u>for</u> our good (versus change happening <u>to</u> us) we evolve. **Yet we cause a revolution within ourselves when we aren't quite sure we can trust the Leader Within. Revolutions kill people. We want evolution within so we can be the positive change in our inside and outside world.**

Mid-Life Genesis

I work with seasoned leaders who have attained success in the conventional way and are looking for a different kind of success; typically, that means tapping into their Visionary SuperPowers (I discuss this more in a later chapter). So what often happens to us in mid-life is that we begin to take a harder look at our priorities. For many, we have our priorities straight when it comes to providing for our families, and at the same time, there is often a calling to live their legacy. The perceived conflict in values is to either put our family's needs at risk by doing something different or do nothing and live with a feeling of emptiness within.

The argument goes like this, "I just can't quit the work I am doing." Maybe not but what *can* you do? When we can see clearly enough to engage our Leader Within we can develop a plan so that we can feel good about supporting our families AND have a fulfilling career. I stand for having both.

We might not have had this problem 100 years ago when we were only living to middle age. Life expectancy in 1916 was: men, 49.6; women, 54.3. How cool that we can start our life over at any minute of the day no matter how old we are. I am asking you to examine your values closely today because values are something we are born with, and they can evolve over time. The older we get the more values we have to align with and balance in our lives.

I work with passionate leaders who have their priorities straight with their families, want to make a positive impact in their world. **Can you imagine what it would be like if everyone took responsibility for their world?** Most of us long for intimacy, connection and purposeful work. **What I can tell you is that the first step to a world like that is for each of us to connect with our Leader Within.**

What if we wake up as leaders and call forth the value in each and every one around us?   By empowering and calling forth the brilliance of others by nourishing and growing our talents and the abilities of others from a place of knowing, there is enough for everyone. Now that's the kind of world we all want, right?   In the next chapter, we will go into detail about the four concepts that successful and fulfilled Business Leaders view as essential to understand to create this world.

CHAPTER THREE
SECRETS TO MAKING EVERY DAY A FRIDAY!

Over the years, I've interviewed hundreds of leaders who have a meaningful and prosperous work-life and asked, what's your secret? As time went on, I analyzed and compiled their answers, which can be reduced to a simple acronym "**ACTT**." **When we are fully Aligned, have a good Crew, know our Transformation and have a Transition plan, we feel fulfilled and for some of us, that feels like Every Day is a Friday.**

"A" is for Alignment

Align yourself with your values

How well aligned are you with your personal values? In the personal values section of this book, you identified your top values and prioritized them. This is one of the first steps in your leadership transformation. **Many leaders never start on something they know they need to do because they fear the conflict between what they want AND what they think their business requires.** Leaders in this situation appear to have two competing values playing a tug-of-war with their desire for a life well-lived and their perception of what's necessary to compete in the business world.

For example, on one hand they want to feel fulfilled by creating a lasting legacy of their own, while on the other hand they don't want to risk financial consistency (oftentimes they don't want to cut staff to maintain their income either). Another example of a conflict in values might be the desire to have freedom of self-expression during the work day, but not wanting to risk your position as senior leader. ("I don't like my manager, but she does a good job. So I need to put up with it and keep my distance from her.") The good news is that your values do NOT have to be mutually exclusive. You can choose to be yourself and be an effective leader at the same time. The question becomes: How do you reconcile your conflicting values? This is where coaching and communication strategies can develop positive change. **How do you get these apparently conflicting sets of goals to reconcile?**

Align yourself with your commitments

Now, let's talk a bit about commitment. You have to put yourself first and know what you will tolerate and what you won't. The distinction that helps me with this is recognizing that self-care is doing what I need to do for myself and hoping it doesn't negatively impact others versus being selfish, which is when I don't give a rat's @$$ about others. So knowing what I will tolerate and what I won't helps me reconcile my values. Your commitments may be something like:

- Self-care
- Quality time with my partner/family
- Work-life flexibility
- Giving back to my community
- Living a prosperous and meaningful life

If you find that your commitments are not properly prioritized, that's okay; we all fall prey to that. It's in these times we realize how compassionate we are with ourselves because it's a perfect time to practice recovering. However, when we misplace our priorities and go on in that condition for too long, we can get stuck in an unhealthy work-life balance. Self-sabotage is very subtle and you only need the light of awareness to start to recover.

Align yourself with your purpose

When we are aligned with our life's purpose and have made a commitment to living our purpose, our confidence builds and our decisions become clearer. *For me, I know that I am a "Fierce Snap*

Inspiring Leaders to Live their Legacy". My life purpose is to inspire a life well-lived. If you feel confused about your purpose, think about a metaphor you resonate with like a bridge or a lighthouse. Perhaps you have people in your life who you trust who can help you identify a metaphor for yourself. After that, think about the impact you want to make based on that metaphor. Once you know your purpose, you can align the gaps in the market (or your world) with the value you bring.

Align yourself with the market

Know YOUR value to the market. This is *KEY!* We must know our value and the value we offer our business. If you are just starting out, know what other industries are paying and why. Include existing projects or special knowledge as well when adding up your value. Further, get to know people of your caliber that are serving your clients in a different way than you are. They might make great partners. Don't be afraid to expand out of your comfort zone! Go to places where you will be the outlier. This is how we get known and grow.

If you're starting a business, know what financial resources you have and need as well as what may be out there available to you. You don't have to fund a business by yourself. Good ideas and a well-written business plan can make it possible to attract investors and grants. The Small Business Administration in the U.S. is a great resource for seed capital and financing, especially for veterans. Also in the U.S., we have an organization called Stand Beside Them that offers complimentary coaching by a certified coach for veterans.

Start-up businesses fail mainly due to poor business planning without credible financial assumptions, or lack good understanding of the business and financial model best suited to the marketplace. This lack of knowledge, and what it really takes to start a business leads to the rather dismal survival rate for new businesses.

If you are an existing Business Owner, what will the market pay for the value you offer? Offer value-based pricing and stop trading dollars for hours. **Most people will pay for outcomes, not hours**. Value-based pricing is more than just cost. Ask yourself what added value you provide and how that compares with the competition.

The one with the lowest price is not always the winner. Quality, service and reputation add real value. In 2008, everyone was saying we were in a recession, YET I kept quoting the same rate I quoted before all the downward pressure on pricing. You know why? My clients saw value in what we offered and the fact that making a business more efficient is one of the solutions to pricing pressure. As a result, I was not compelled to participate in the recession.

Align yourself with the value you bring

It doesn't matter if you have built your business from the ground up and are making millions of dollars, or you are just starting out. You are valuable in ways you don't even yet realize. One way to get clear on the value you bring others is by asking them (make sure you want to hear their answer though). Know the value you bring to your customers, employees and even your family. **If we don't value ourselves, we can't possibly recognize how special or unique we are, and we will painfully base our measure of success on numbers or how our boss sees us.**

If you are transitioning away from a profitable business you've built, *know the value you contributed to the business and make sure that your successor can sustain or increase the value. In other words, who* really is the best fit versus who you might feel obligated to transition the business over to. The bottom line is we must be aligned with the value we provide, or we will lose confidence in what we authentically offer and settle for less than what we deserve.

Align your customer gaps with your strengths

We will talk about strengths a little later, what we call SuperPowers. However, whatever your strengths, it's best to position ourselves as the go-to person for a particular problem to be solved in our business or market. We need to have an understanding of the pain of the people we are serving. What does your customer see, hear and feel, and (most importantly) value? If you're a B2B (Business to Business Company), what does your *customer's customer* see? *You must be able to see yourself through the eyes of your customer. A little later in this book, I will show you how to draw a model that can show you the touch points between you and your customer called the "Line of Sight Model." But for now, here is an example of my ideal client's gaps:*

My Ideal Client "Avatar"

1. *Creative, financially successful Business Leaders between 35-55 years old who need to refocus on their purpose and legacy as a leader. They have a team of employees counting on them for guidance and direction. My second Client Avatars are entrepreneurs wanting to make money from their passion.*

2. *Most of them are married or in a committed relationship and have kids either from their current or prior marriage.*

3. *They have a high workload coupled with strong family priorities. They are financially successful and yet there is still something lacking in the area of work-life fulfillment.*

4. *They are hesitant to open up or just don't talk to people at work about a clear plan for fear of feeling exposed or being placated.*

5. *They are taking a hard look at the life they are living. They want a lifelong legacy, yet they in many ways do life and work alone.*

Where they go for info:

- *They typically watch CNN or MSNBC, browse their company website or LinkedIn profiles and groups to see how their peers are doing, rarely go to Facebook. They may or may not have a Google Plus account. They will go to webinars for personal and professional development reasons. They read the Economist, Bloomberg Business Week, CIO magazine, Entrepreneur magazine, and go to TEDx conferences.*

Feelings:

- *They feel frustrated, unsatisfied, under pressure, conflicted, lonely. They are struggling with making healthy choices while filled with various urges fighting that process. They feel uneasy; their parents are older or have passed away, and now they need more answers than they ever have. They are afraid, yet dream of leaving the career they have worked so hard to build. This could also include leaving their family, having an affair, drinking or eating more than they should. They feel the pressure to have all the answers and be the breadwinner in their families. They are angry with their partners/families for putting undue pressure on them.*

Wants:

- *Flexibility, freedom to fully self-express their legacy, fulfillment and financial security.*

- *To enjoy the ride—enjoy life now, even while building something to which they aspire.*

- *They want to make wise choices while coming out of a midlife crisis and into a happier life, AND they don't want to lose the good they have achieved in their home and work lives.*

- *They want adventure, and they don't want to have financial trouble or raise a red flag with partners. They want a fun, rewarding business with sustainable results.*

Needs:

- *Need to feel alive, inspired and full of hope that it is possible to have a work-life that supports their dreams and lifestyle (family), AND they can put themselves on the road to get there.*

- *Focus on what they want and not have a big blow-up in their family over it.*

- *Need to detach with compassion from time-intensive issues or family/work drama.*

- *Need to know how to achieve fulfillment and ensure financial security for their family.*

- *To know how to handle their feelings without self-destructing.*

- *A safe place to process their next steps in their business, travel the world, go back to school, or open yet another business.*

- *Maximize their time by working with other successful Business Leaders.*

What are their gaps that I can help them with?

- *They need an objective set of eyes and ears to help them identify what's next for them, so that they can rebrand themselves as leaders. They need to attain a positive mindset and have practical tools to achieve these wants and needs.*

- *Inspired and equipped to have a work-life that supports their legacy and meet the financial needs of their family.*

Promise/Outcome:

- *By the time you leave this leadership program you will have the tools and mindset you need to have a fulfilling and prosperous work-life that does more than pay the bills.*

This turns into my stump speech:

- *"Are you ready for a Super Team that you can rely on to be there for you always? The **ACTT** Leadership Program provides an inspiring and informative space for Business Leaders (C-level executives, Business Owners and entrepreneurs) to have a meaningful and prosperous work-life that does more than pay the bills."*

Align your strengths with a strong business model

One of my clients is a franchise owner but his Leadership strength (SuperPower) is in being a Visionary. Operating a day-to-day franchise with little to no room for personal creativity is the worst industry for him. He is frustrated because he is not aligning his Leadership SuperPowers with his business model. Now, the key to being a Visionary is to **sell your creations first before building them entirely.** Then understand how you can multiply your creations so you're not constantly recreating from scratch. Another example is if you are a people person (Relational SuperPower), how can you magnify other people's products or services? Because you may not be naturally inclined to create new products and services. A Relational Leader needs a Visionary and vice-versa; we will cover this later when we talk about Crew.

Align yourself with your assumptions

Business Leaders also fail when they have a partnership and falsely assume that their colleagues or business partners have the same work preferences or success measures. When Business Leaders work together in partnerships, a huge benefit is to work with a coach on how you will operate together. A good coach can hear the assumptions that each partner is making and help build a solid partnership plan to stop problems before they start. (Questions the coach may ask are, for example: What roles will we play? How will decisions be made? How will we function together in a conflict?).

If you're a Business Leader in transition, there is often an imaginary conversation that hasn't happened yet. Some clients say, "Nina, I want my work-life dream but I need cash flow. I need health insurance. My spouse has an expectation about the way we live and transitioning now would put all that at risk." To which I reply, **"What assumptions are you making about the way your spouse might prioritize *your* work life?"** When we let our anxiety rule the conversations in our mind, we challenge our natural state to stay in wonder.

One important note: make sure your significant other is on board and supportive of your dream and can accept the risk. However, if they aren't in it 99.99%, listen to what they have to say with an open mind. After all, they may know you better than you know yourself. We all have a blind spot when it comes to our own way of operating. Indeed, their observations—if they are honest—may raise valid concerns, which may in turn help lead us to better preparation and greater chances of success. Sometimes this may mean an honest conversation about finances. What we really need versus what we want. **Many spouses won't agree to their partner starting a business or making any other career move if they don't feel that their partner is completely committed to making the change.**

How Aligned Are You?

The fact that you are reading this book tells me your Leader Within is talking to you and you are listening, so to explore that further:

- How important is having a meaningful and prosperous work-life that does more than pay the bills to you?

- What is your vision for your business and your life?

- What talents and skills do you have that set you apart from others in your field?

- How do you use your talents to help your business do what it does best?

- What gaps in the world are you inspired to fill?

- How does the mission for your business align with your life's purpose?

- How does your business help you realize your life's work?

"C" is for Crew

The whole is greater than the sum of its parts. -Aristotle

Let's go way, way back in time for a moment. Think about how a ship in the 18th century operated. Both the Captain and the Crew have one common goal—smooth sailing! The Crew is reliant on the Captain to operate skillfully and make good decisions, and the Captain is reliant on the Crew to fulfill their roles. Each member on the ship is a leader who relies on the other leaders to perform their roles for the good of everyone. In fact, a Captain could at any time be demoted if the Crew felt that the Captain did not have their best interests in mind, or was too humble or too arrogant.

So, you can see that the Crew and the Captain have an inter-dependent relationship with one another, what we call in Corporate America a "Shared Vision." With all of our technology, we have a false sense of independence, and although we don't "need" one another for survival, we still could all use a little smooth sailing in our lives by acknowledging our interdependence.

Being the youngest by nine years in my family with parents who fought all the time, I ran from almost any form of a good Crew. As I grew older, I wanted to have good Crew. I just didn't know how. At 26 years old I made a decision to find out how to be in good relationships. I went to any meeting, any class that would teach me the life skills I didn't learn growing up. One of the most impactful programs, for me, is a 12-step program called Al-anon. The only requirement of Al-anon membership is that we have been affected by someone else's drinking. Know anyone like that? Through Al-anon, I found a loving sponsor, Lillian, who has become like a mom to me. A sponsor is like a mentor for those of you who are not familiar with the 12-steps. Lillian eventually "adopted" me into her Italian family. I am so grateful to have Lillian in my life. She taught me so much about being and staying with a good healthy Crew. In fact, if it weren't for her, I would not be who I am today.

Modern Day Crew

We cannot solve our problems with the same level of thinking that created them. -Albert Einstein

A Crew is different than a "team" or "employees," and, of course, can be different from your family of origin. A Crew is made up of people who are 99.99% committed to your success. You can be vulnerable with your Crew because they have no hidden agenda and they will point you to forward-focused proactive action. They are objective and have no other interest other than in your success. They know that there is enough for everyone and will do whatever is necessary to ensure your success.

Having accountability as part of your Crew's intention, much like that of a mastermind group's, is crucial during transition. We need to be around objective people who are committed to us and have something to offer us, so that we can gain the fortitude to change course if things aren't going the way we like. It is critical that Business Leaders realize they don't have to go it alone. You can have a Crew in the form of coaches, mentors and other Business Leaders. I learned that by being part of and leading mastermind groups, I could multiply my time and effectiveness by working with a Crew, especially those who have complementary skills. We also need to be around people we can trust, so that we can gain the fortitude to change course if things aren't going the way we like.

For example, I am a Visionary (my Leadership SuperPower); I love to create new things and I need someone to keep my feet on the ground. With the number of projects I take on, I need a member of my Crew to remind me of my cash flow and other practical and administrative requirements. I call that person a Logical Leader. It doesn't mean that Visionaries aren't logical. It just means that Visionaries need someone who can see how the vision can be accomplished. In fact, learning to delegate and trust others is key to becoming a successful Business Leader regardless of your SuperPower.

If you are starting your own business and need clients, or you work within an organization and are trying to create positive change, the most efficient and effective way to do so is to align with a good Crew that serves the same customer you do or has similar goals. For example, in my first company, Metaspire Consulting, I aligned with a process management software company. Why? Because my team was made up of process architects, Six Sigma Black-Belts and leadership coaches. We had no interest in selling technology and the technology company had little interest in serving their clients in the way that we could. In the same way when I was a global project manager at Amex, I was responsible for the communication and training for a Worldwide Technology change involving project managers. I couldn't do that alone so I met with key directors and vice-presidents (gatekeepers) in each department so that I could ensure we were all aligned on the importance of the change, the benefit of the change, and the impact of the change.

Remember that as the Captain of your own ship, you must make a conscious choice to positively impact others in what you are trying to achieve, and it all starts with knowing your Crew. Like I said earlier, everyone has a Leader Within (Captain). We are born with that capacity and the more we listen to that part of ourselves, the more effective we are as leaders. If we don't listen to this part of ourselves we get resentful, pissed off, or we go numb. Don't let that happen to you!

This is Your Captain Speaking

Who is your Captain? Not your boss, not your customer, not your partner, and not your mama! What do you call that part of yourself that leads you from within towards the fulfillment of your life purpose? There are no rules dictating that your Captain be human or of this earth. Let your imagination move you to a safe place (maybe a place you would go as a child, or a favorite vacation spot or perhaps a place not of this world) and when you are there, invite your Captain to join you. Quiet your mind long enough to listen to your Captain. Find out what your Captain wants for you. Ask how you can connect with your Captain more easily. Your Leadership Presence is crucial to knowing your Leader Within (Captain) and those on your inside Crew (you know, those voices in your mind). When your Crew Members are aligned internally with your idea of fulfillment, it's much easier to connect with the world around you.

Many of us can't talk to our colleagues at work—they may not be objective, and some of us can't talk to our families because although they love us, they might not know what we should do professionally.

So we end up doing things ourselves, wanting to make good decisions, yet we isolate ourselves, thinking, once again, "I should know this," or, "I'll Google it," or the most famous one, "If you want something done right, do it yourself."

Well, Captain, Who is Your Crew?

The Personal Fulfillment Chain

If you focus on being fulfilled, you will be happier at work and happier at home. When you're fulfilled, you see the world differently and the world is inspired by your happiness. When employees are happy, they will have one of the most important tools necessary to make your customers happy, particularly in a service-based business. This is evident in the service profit chain; happy employees make happy customers, which in turn creates loyal clients, which in turn creates sustainable sales, which ultimately creates happy business share-holders. The USA is moving away from the routine grunt work of the industrial age. Much more of our economy is moving into services where "service" is the main element of providing value.

Having a Crew not only provides a trusted expert advisory board, it also provides tremendous value by sharing what other leaders are doing right in their businesses. I can't imagine my life without strong people around me raising the bar. I am sure my life would be okay, but it wouldn't be great. I know the power of mastermind groups and leadership programs. I feel so blessed to be able to lead them. Here's the bottom line, you know that someone is part of your Crew when they respond in the following ways:

1. I know what you want, Captain, and I will do my part in helping you get there.

2. 1 + 1 = chicken; meaning, when we get together and effectively collaborate, positive results beyond our wildest dreams will appear.

3. "We-speak," coming from the "How will we...." perspective. Which often means that we must be brave enough to:

   a. "Talk about the elephant in the room" in a kind way, and:

   b. Practice "Go-Set-Ready" (starting as soon as possible—in a likely awkward fashion and, of course, being okay with failing, because that means we learned).

Successful leaders learn to share their achievement of attaining their dream by helping others attain theirs. **Your Crew will help keep you focused on the fact that your business is not all about you and your needs.** Your Crew will understand your vision and goals and help keep you focused on your vision, both for yourself and others. They know, as do all students of business, that happy employees and happy clients will mean a happy you.

We have seen great results in our Leadership Program using the book, *"Co-Active Leadership: Five Ways to Lead,"* by Henry and Karen Kimsey-House. We often point our clients to this book when we ask them to do the following exercise. By visually identifying your current Crew Members, this exercise will reveal where other Crew Members are needed to complement your leadership strengths (or what we call Leadership SuperPowers).

Your Crew

Take a moment now and answer the following questions. Once you are complete, write the names of your Crew Members on the appropriate position on your ship!

1. Who in your life will tell you about what you already know but don't want to admit needs to change?

2. Who is your Captain? Not your boss, not your client, not your life partner, and not your mama!

3. What do you call that part of yourself that leads you from within towards the fulfillment of your life purpose?

4. Who in your life provides you a "big picture view" of what is happening (Leader from the Field)?

5. Who in your life possesses the professional tools necessary to move you forward? Or who do you admire and want to be more like, e.g. a mentor (Leader from the Front)?

6. Who in your life are you so close to in thought that you can't remember who said what? Who in your life serves

the same customers or has the same interests you do but in a different way (Leader from Beside)?

7. Who in your life works as an emotionally supportive person, e.g. a coach (Leader from Behind) offering you thought provoking questions?

Your Crew Ship Exercise

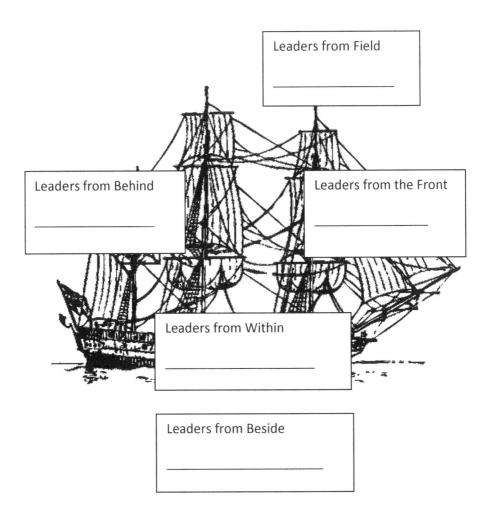

Leaders from Field
_____

Leaders from Behind
_____

Leaders from the Front
_____

Leaders from Within
_____

Leaders from Beside
_____

Your Inside Crew (Leaders from Within)

When I was about seventeen, my friend Donna and I decided to travel to the **cornerstone musical festival in Chicago**. I was **complaining** about something or other, like any happy teenager often does (sarcasm). **Donna listened quietly**, and as she gently **rolled down her window**, said, *"Nina, you just need to be a whole person."* I was like *"What? What the What??"* A bunch of questions ran through my mind.

For instance, "What does that even mean? Which part of me is she talking about?" Ever since I was little, I knew that I had many sides of myself, yet I had no idea what she was talking about. This conversation stayed with me for years as I studied personal and professional development.

Have you seen Pixar's movie, *Inside Out?* This movie is a dream come true for transformational coaches such as myself. At last, the word is out in a big way that we ALL have conversations in our mind, especially when we are making decisions, or when someone rubs us the wrong way, am I right? Although Pixar's movie expresses the inside voices as emotions, there is much more under the surface. This work of sub-personalities has been around for years. For example, the brilliant author, John Rowan, wrote about the different parts of our minds in the book, *Subpersonalities: The People Inside Us*. The book explains how different parts of ourselves come forward based on the situation at hand.

Although we have encouraging voices in our minds, the toughest voice for me to make peace with is the voice of the internal judge that says, "Not good enough," or, "I am not wanted." On the other side of the boardroom is my Leader Within who knows that in order to make peace, I have to learn what's good about having an internal judge. During a recent speaking event, I talked about how not feeling good enough can often mean a value of quality is being overly expressed and not feeling wanted means that I've placed an overly high value on relationships. **Over the years, I continue to learn that a whole person is someone that can rally all those voices in their mind and make conscious healthy choices.** I hope that this has sparked some differing conversations in your mind! Either way, I'd like to propose a thought-provoking question: **"Who's running your Inside Crew right now?"**

So, like I said earlier, at any one time, especially when making decisions or holding a boundary, there are opposing voices in our minds expressing different needs. I call this our inside Crew. When we identify the values each inner Crew Member is trying to express, we can come to a conscious decision. We still have external circumstances to deal with and yet should have a feeling of peace inside. This isn't always easy to achieve on our own. Oftentimes, we get hijacked by our own thought processes and end up stuck, stymied. This is why an "external" Crew is vital in times of transition. We must have mirrors (coach, mentor, mastermind group, etc.) to help us "see" what we are lacking.

I'll give you an example: recently, one of my teenage step-daughters had been actively resistant to doing her regular chores. If you're a parent, especially a step-parent (fighting the evil step-mother persona), you understand the conflict and know that teenagers need consistency. My husband (her father) had been traveling extensively, and so I was home with our two daughters and had to address the situation head on.

The first voice in my mind said, "She's only doing what she knows to do. Just ignore her while she is here. She doesn't listen to you anyway." Another voice said, "I don't care. I don't want to be near her." Yet a third said, "You're a coach, you should know how to figure this out." As a coach, I have high expectations for myself; however, I needed help on this one!

As I met with our family coach, Lucetta, I let each voice speak for a moment. I found that my values were conflicted. One value I have is to be a supportive partner to my husband by helping him while he is away, another is called self-care, and a third honors my profession by practicing what I preach. I realized that I am a step-mother, not a step-on mother. I learned that it would be familiar for me to just let her do what she wants to do and not enforce her chores while I am with her. But it's not effective. If we want effective, we need to get in touch with our healthy inner teenager that is willing to risk the familiar for a better way. Make sense? By holding our boundaries as a family, my relationship with my step-daughter has never been better. For me it stems from taking responsibility for my world.

Another example of navigating my inner Crew is when I decided to concentrate on leadership coaching. One voice said, "No, Nina, stay with this consulting business. You're making a lot of money and you are your own boss. You don't know what's around the corner." A second voice said, "If I were to die now, what would my life have meant?" You see, two conflicting values: one that says, "Stay financially successful," another that says, "Be in service to others." So I had to sit with those voices until a third butted in (my healthy teenager) that said, "What if I could have both?" Thus, BusinessCoachingOnDemand.com was started, offering coaching, mentoring and leadership groups for business leaders.

Typically, when we feel stuck it's helpful to be around people who assume you are naturally creative, resourceful, and whole. In this way, they can help you identify your conflicting values and develop a strong plan for moving forward. **The bottom line is if your home or work environment expresses values other than your own personal values, it's time to do something different.**

Inside Crew Mind Map

Creating our own unique, inside Crew (Leaders from Within) mind map will allow us to gain a stronger awareness and understanding of our world within. In this exercise, you will have the opportunity to look inward and reflect on your internal beliefs, assumptions, and values, as well as to expand your knowledge of just what leadership is and is not. Identifying your intrinsic core values will propel you forward in your personal and work-life. By focusing on our constructive attributes, possibilities become clearer, and the celebration of the positive outcomes that are certain to follow is more likely to occur.

Some of our clients identify their inside Crew Members by their values; for example, Adam the Appreciator, Alice the Adventurer, Move-it Molly, Slow-it-Down Sally, Creative Connie, Curious Chris, Larry the Listener, Intuitive Nina, and Rational Robert. Or you can examine the different stages of development that you carry with you today: e.g. Little Nina, Teenager Tina, or Grumpy Granny, etc. You may notice that Crew Members often balance one another so an adventurous side of you may need to have a conversation with the rational side. Ultimately, all voices are inside of us to serve our highest good. The key is building our objective observer (Leader Within) in order to honor each part.

For this exercise you will need a blank piece of paper, or better yet, a poster board. When creating your Inside Crew Member mind map, think about what you might name your Leader Within. This is an opportunity for you to identify the attributes that stand out in your internal guidance system. Consider including branches, such as events or triggers that call forth your Leader Within. Perhaps there are symbols, metaphors, quotes or images that you want to include. Remember to also include what makes you feel fulfilled, some of your core values, and what you know about your life purpose(s).

Tips:

- Breathe. Slow down and be quiet enough to hear your Leader Within.

- Be Aware. Notice your thoughts, feelings and assumptions, and notice how your Leader Within responds to these things. Don't get hijacked by critical voices that don't serve you.

- Think about doing this exercise with a coach or friend that can help keep you on track (they won't have the same critical voices in their head about you).

- Each mind map is unique. Yours will be exactly as it should be for today. Enjoy the process and have fun!

- Extra Credit. What's it like knowing you have a Leader Within (internal positive guidance system)? Do you feel this knowing in some particular place within your body?

Inside Crew Mind Map Example:

In one example, my client identified his Leader Within (Captain) as the "Loopy Flow." He showed how he values the journey, not the destination, by drawing continuous circles. Also he listed his core values and created ownership by stating, "I am grounded and clear." Finally, he identified with several versions of his life purpose.

A Closer Look at "C" for Crew

It's lonely at the top," but only if you don't align yourself with a capable and committed Crew.

As discussed earlier, it's critical that Business Leaders realize they don't have to go it alone. You can have a Crew in the form of coaches, mentors, partners, and other Business Leaders. These folks have an idea of the various distractions that can impact your leadership. Although your family may be emotionally supportive, consider how much they can speak to what is happening in your particular industry and situation.

Those who report to you in the organization are apt to be politically correct and focused on their own agenda rather than to be honest and tell you what you should know. Often, one of the more prevalent mistakes Business Leaders make is when they surround themselves with people too similar to themselves. **This is solved with the magic of the development of a mastermind group or a "Crew" of people who have a variety of business and leadership experience and can empathize and strategize with you.**

The truth is that often, as "the boss," it's difficult to get real, honest feedback from the people you are paying. Unfortunately, many leaders have learned their styles from limited examples, and have very limited contrasting viewpoints to challenge them.

Your Customer

The idea of a customer (or client) being on your Crew is a progressive one. I mean how vulnerable can you really be with a client right? In coaching, staying reserved when a client is processing is called "self-management." However, without our clients we don't have a business, so why not put them on the ship with the rest of our Crew?

If we're in business, we need to really understand our customer because we need one another. If we're smart, we'll anticipate what they want or need before they even ask. Once we have an understanding of how our customer thinks, feels, acts, we then "hold the space" in our minds and in our communications for them to respond. When you think about your customer, it should conjure up a single person. This is not to say all your clients will fit into one box perfectly. However, once you've identified your customer, place an object or photo that represents your vision of *your ideal customer where you can be reminded of who you serve every day.*

Your Customer Assessment

Before completing the exercises below, review the "My Ideal Client" section of this book as an example to help you identify your perfect client:

- Who are they? What do they feel now? Want? Need? What Gaps or Pains do they have? What is the ultimate outcome they want by working with you?

- What can you promise your customer?

- How will you get in front of them?

- Where do they go? What do they do?

- What are neighboring (like) industries that serve them?

The People You Work With

What about *your* company? What would it be like if 10% more of the people in your organization worked together like a Crew? The following models represent two different organizational systems. The first model shows a Misaligned Organizational System and the second is an Aligned System resulting in an empowered team. Notice in the Misaligned System, there is very little open communication resulting in conflicting goals, unnecessary hand-offs and, of course, burdened teams.

Misaligned Organizational System

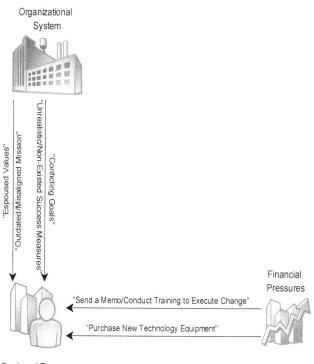

Aligned Organizational System

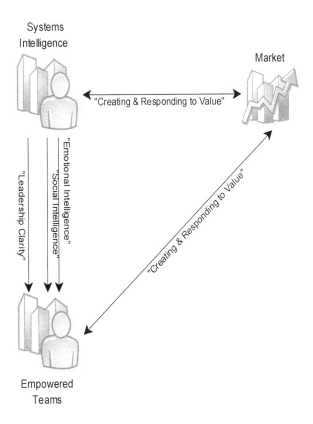

On the other hand, an Aligned Organization centralizes around an empowered team who create and respond to market value and the market responds to the value of their team e.g. they listen and anticipate their customers' needs and are in tune with market changes.

Keeping the two models in mind, which most closely represents your organization today? What might you do to create a stronger positive impact within your work-environment?

As a Business Leader, you need to develop good habits that support quality work practices. A "real company" has formal and informal communications and yet is smart enough to listen to employees who have direct contact with their customers. This helps to insure employee and customer engagement, resulting in consistency, quality and improved productivity. If your employees are making up their own processes and procedures, the first step conscious Business Leaders take is to get curious about *why* this may be happening. Perhaps your employees and customers know more than you do at this point in time. Your job as a leader is to build an empowered Crew.

Successful leaders know that they must let go of working IN the business and commit to working ON the business. This means leaders need to create their own company leaders who think and act like Business Owners. That doesn't mean they need to be *exactly* like the decision maker. Studies have shown that diversity in leadership helps by bringing a variety of experiences and insights into the mix. If you want to have the most productive time at work, listen to the person that is most qualified to make a decision, not the person with the most formal authority.

One way to do that is to build trust. The most difficult yet important thing we can do when building trust is to hold people accountable to their word and agreed-upon success measures. Without properly supported two-way communications, it's impossible to build an organization to which you can delegate responsibilities. One of the more productive tasks you can do in your career is to learn not to be a micromanager, yet still hold employees accountable. Micromanaging holds your employees back and can kill motivation because you aren't acknowledging their Leader Within.

People want feedback on how well they are doing their jobs. Financial and business metrics allow for an *objective measurement of performance.* Today, leaders are moving toward inclusion and transparency; a far cry from the days of rigid hierarchy and an environment of fear. As we all know, good jobs require new skills, and top talent for many jobs is in short supply. This is forcing leaders to take leadership development much more seriously.

Empowered Crew

The following graphic depicts the activities and events that would support an Empowered Crew or an effective team. You will notice the "closed loop" communication activities between the Leader, the Customer and the Crew.

If you work in an existing organization as a C-level leader, it is crucial to get to know those with whom you work. One meaningful way to connect is to work together to map out how you will work together as a Crew.

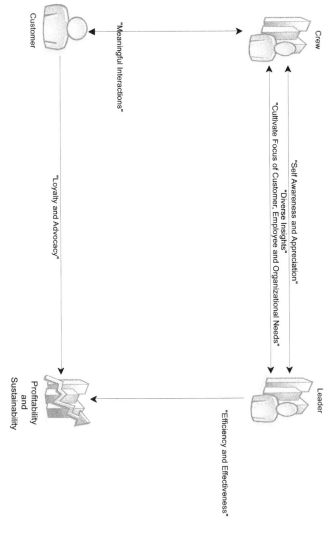

Business Interaction Model (BIM)

The Business Interaction Model or (BIM) depicts internal and external organizational interactions. It is typically used for identifying major business deliverables and hand-offs between departments. This oftentimes will help facilitate a conversation around best practices and establishes what is required at a more tactical level to accomplish goals.

One of the most important functions in successfully operating a business is to know how the business will interact with other departments inside and outside the company. Why? Because if we don't know how we are going to operate together, how will we serve our customer?

On the next page you will notice a BIM showing how Research and Development and Manufacturing act as Suppliers to Marketing, Inbound Sales, Operations and Distribution. All of these departments work together so that the Customer group of Early Adopters can be offered new products based on anticipating Customer requirements. It also notes that Competitors will be advertising their products to our Customers as well. Although this is a high-level model, it can be used to understand how we are fulfilling our customer's needs.

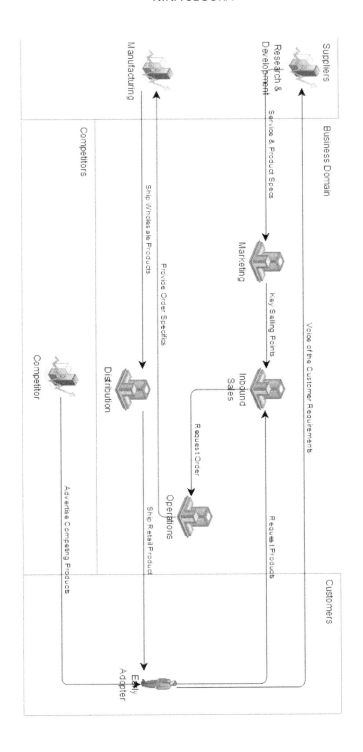

Process Model

Here is the thing; as a trained business process architect, I can tell you there are only a handful of different process types in an organization. On the following page you will see an example of a Process Model showing typical major processes for most businesses. Depending on the company size, there could be hundreds, even thousands of activities under each blue process bubble. See more process category examples in Chapter 9.

NINA SEGURA

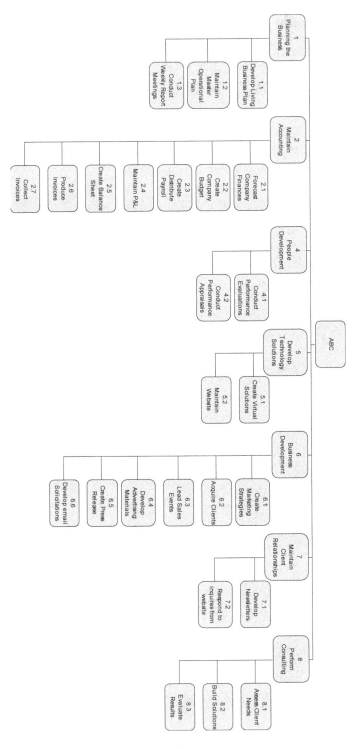

Building an enterprise-wide Process Model will help frame any departmental goals and, if you're starting a business, help your business plan come alive (not one that is just a template of what you would like to have happen, rather an organic plan that is followed, benchmarked and flexible enough to fit any situation when there is change).

In fact, there are two vital parts of a business plan that no one talks about: a Transformation Strategy and a Transition Plan. Let me tell you, running a business is a huge time compressor. The years pass by so quickly, if you don't constantly have your "eye on the prize," you and your company can become disoriented and even get lost. Your Crew needs to know where you are headed. That brings us to the next letter in our acronym: "T."

> *How does one become a butterfly? You have to want to learn to fly so much that you are willing to give up being a caterpillar.*
> *-Trina Paulus*

"T" Stands for Transformation Strategy

Perhaps what has always fascinated me about butterflies is that I understand what it's like for my insides to feel like goo. In all seriousness, the reason I mention this is because Transformation is easier felt than explained. The most famous analogy about Transformation is metamorphosis, of course. Transformation is very different from being in a transition because we can't make Transformation happen for ourselves (or those around us, for that matter). However, we can:

- Make a conscious choice to change.

- Take action towards positive change.

- Commit to a time and space for Transformation to happen.

- Be introspective and vulnerable with someone you trust.

- Take responsibility for your part in what's around you.

- Work with a change agent like a mentor, coach, and or therapist.

- Join a mastermind or leadership group.

Check off which of the bullets above you are committed to doing.

So, why is Transformation such an important part of being a leader? Because every leader who has made a positive impact in this world has a Transformational story about his or her journey. Further, if you are a Business Owner, and especially a coach, being able to articulate your Transformation story to a prospective client is critical in having that client know, like and trust you (a good beginning for any relationship, wouldn't you say?). I could write another book on Transformation alone, however, for the purposes of this book, I must share one additional vital component of Transformation called, "The Stake," based on the book with the same name written by Henry Kimsey-House.

Your Leadership Stake

A Leadership Stake has two components. The first is what we believe and the second is the anticipated outcome that will occur based on our belief. This concept really clicked for me as Leadership Coach Rick Tamlyn gave the following example, "Jesus is the only way to heaven."

The Leadership Stake for BusinessCoachingOnDemand.com is, "When we are fulfilled at work, we are happier at home, and when we are happy at home, the world is a better place." I offer two more examples from my colleague, Emilie Steele Giustozzi, IT Leader and Professional Coach. First, "Everything is better when everyone buys into the effort and contributes." ("Stone Soup Concept.") Emilie's second stake is, "People will engage from the heart when they know it is safe to do so." (Her "Safe Harbor" stake.)

Putting your "leadership stake" in the "ground" at minimum will boost your sales process, and at best will transform an entire culture.

So first, here is what I learned about transformation specific to the sales process. Many of us, especially coaches, have been trained to give "free sample sessions," which is really just a gateway for the prospective client to understand what can occur for them (transformation). The top two things that help people transform are powerful questions that tap into their Leader Within and secondly transformational stories about how the product or service will provide an ultimate outcome for the prospect.

For example, say we start with a problem in the form of a question, "What do you know about your life purpose?" After listening deeply to their ultimate outcome, I share my transformation story based on my leadership stake. If the story resonates and I think I am a good fit to help the prospect with their gaps, I invite them to take one positive action step toward their ultimate outcome, which is to sign up for my leadership program.

Imagine what our world would be like if everyone realized how similar our DNA is to every other person on our planet through stories? After that realization might we then ask ourselves the question, how might we get along better cousin? This is why committing to making a positive impact AND understanding the impact we have on others is so important. Because sometimes, we think that we have positively impacted those around us, and THEY don't feel that way at all. Many corporations offer 360-degree feedback sessions for their leaders to address this Transformation Strategy.

In my programs, leaders take an assessment before the program and then the same assessment is taken after the program. In this way my clients can see the tangible progress they are making. I do this because often times when we are doing the deep inner work that Transformation requires, we forget what we were like before we committed to Transformation in the first place. Which brings me to another important Transformational ingredient—coaching!

What Real Coaches Do

Real coaches create transformational experiences. Typically, Transformation *results* in an external change that could be making a big decision about your work environment or simply exhibiting a new attitude. This book is only one way for you to have a Transformation experience. Further, the work you do in this book works even better when you are working with a real coach.

I use the term real coach because coaching is not a regulated industry and for those of us that went through the training, the group and one-on-one supervisions, engaged in hundreds of paid coaching hours and the written and oral international exams, we are trained "Real Coaches." This can be much, much different from those calling themselves coaches in Natural Awakenings ads at Whole Foods. The only requirement for these folks is to be able to afford the ad.

In case you didn't know, coaching differs from consulting. Coaching is a thought-provoking objective conversation to bring out your Leader Within. A consultant or business mentor has technical expertise that can solve business problems. This is the gap that my company BusinessCoachingOnDemand.com fills. We provide a practical business, leadership and management tools and create transformational "spaces" during our leadership retreats.

Coaching helps clients figure out what they want, what they are committed to, and how much change they are willing to create in themselves and in their organizations. Oftentimes clients hire coaches because they know there is something better for themselves. They may be starting, expanding or transitioning from their current role. In other cases, people hire coaches because they are ready to fulfill a lifelong desire. Most clients just want a stronger sense of fulfillment.

As a coach, one of the first things we do is clearly define our client's values, strengths and success measures. For example, during the Coaching Discovery Process you may state that you want to make a lot of money. But when your coach probes deeper, it turns out that you really want the flexibility you think money can buy.

In fact, the most common complaint I hear from Business Leaders is their lack of free time. **We all have the same amount of time. It isn't a time issue, it's a prioritization issue.** Sometimes that can be solved by knowing when to delegate tasks to others and hold them accountable. That is a good example of how a trained coach can bridge the gap between business and leadership development. A good coach will cost between $500 and $10,000 a month. Now, for some of you who think that is a lot of money, consider how much it might be worth it for you to resolve some of the things that keep you up at night?

In Co-Active Coaching, we have this "thing" called "Level 3 Listening." It's a practical AND mystical "thing" that happens when we are deeply connected to everything around us; when we are so completely in sync with the person who is speaking, we aren't quite sure who said what. It is at that point when our ego ceases that something far better than any of us can imagine alone happens.

This is why I believe mastermind groups are re-surging in popularity—to provide us the objective and qualified set of eyes and ears that can get us to where we want to be faster and better than we could alone. **Unfortunately, especially for those of us in midlife, we forget to invest in our own self-development and growth. We think that somehow our self-investment takes away from our priorities, our time with our families, our future.** On the other hand, what if exploring the question inside of us is far better than sending that one last email or taking that one last business trip? Coaching provides us with structured time to think clearly in an objective environment. Other benefits include:

1. Peace of Mind

   a. Perspective when facing life-changing decisions

   b. Reduction in stress and conflict

   c. Improved work-life balance

2. Clarity

   a. Greater awareness of opportunities

b. Leading from your strengths

c. Improved ability to make great decisions under pressure

Don't just take it from me; listen as Joe Drogo, CPCC, ACC, Soulistic Life Coach from Orlando, Florida and I interview a few respected coaches in our industry. But, before we get started, check out their backgrounds.

Cynthia Loy Darst, CPCC, ORSCC, MCC & David Loy Darst, CPCC, ORSCC, PCC

Cynthia began her coaching career in 1992 and founded The Inspiration Point in 1997. Known as a passionate pioneer in the coaching industry, Cynthia is inspiring and playful, working with her clients to move past limitations and into action. She is also a guest expert and "life coach" for a growing number of TV shows. Cynthia was once named "One of the Top Ten Most Influential Coaches in the U.S."

A coach of coaches, Cynthia served as President of The Association of Coach Organizations (ACTO) in 2012-2013. In addition, she was instrumental in starting the International Coach Federation in 1995 and was the first Ethics Chair of the Professional & Personal Coaches Assoc. (Which later merged with the International Coach Federation).

A Certified Professional Co-Active Coach and a Certified Relationship & Systems Coach, Cynthia is also recognized as a Master Certified Coach from the International Coach Federation and a Board Certified Coach from CCE. She and David Darst are also on the faculty of CTI (The Coaches Training Institute) and CRR Global (The Center for Right Relationship). As a side note, Cynthia has been my coach for years and has positively impacted my life, my family and my business in ways that are too numerous to count. I can only imagine what it might be like for her at some point to have a glimpse of how she has made our world a better place.

Her partner, David Loy Darst, joined the Inspiration Point in 1999. Since then he has trained and worked with more than a thousand coaches, both in one-on-one coaching and relationship and systems coaching. Referred to as a "Renaissance Man," he brings a strong and eclectic background to his coaching. He was a master carpenter and furniture designer, worked in the entertainment industry—both in front and behind the scenes, as well as 10 years of experience with working with people in recovery of alcohol and drug addiction.

Whether working with a piece of wood or a human being in the midst of a struggle, David has a gift for spotting and coaxing forth the beauty within. David is the past President of the Los Angeles Chapter of the International Coach Federation, a Board Certified Coach, and is a member of the ICF. He travels worldwide from his home base in Los Angeles. Below is an excerpt of our interview with them.

Nina: The topic comes up often about what real coaches do, and we consider you real coaches, so what do you offer?

Cynthia: That's a good question because what we do, in my opinion, is lean into the wisdom of our client. A lot of people think that coaches are going to tell you what to do. They're going to say, "Here's what you're going to do with your life," but that's not what a coach does. A coach finds out who this person is and what their wisdom is, and leads them to their mastery in life to pull out the very best in them.

David: You've probably heard this before but it's a side-by-side conversation, like the way we are sitting right now, that's what I'm doing with my clients. We're sitting side by side; I'm asking questions so that they can look at what's ahead of them in a different way than what they'd normally see on their own.

Cynthia: That's pretty much it!

Joe: Yet, it's still an intimate relationship, if we can call it a "relationship," yes?

Cynthia: Absolutely! In the world of coaching, particularly Co-Active Coaching, which is what is taught by the Coaches Training Institute, what we want to do is have both the coach and the client empowered in the coaching relationship.

David: In my day it was, "Here's how I got my life to be great; why don't you try what I did?"

Cynthia: See, that might be a kind of mentoring, it might be a kind of consulting, but it's not coaching. Not by the ICF definition of coaching, the International Coach Federation, and it is certainly not the model that the Coaches Training Institute offers.

Joe: So what do you see for the future of coaching?

Cynthia: What I'm noticing is we're getting work left, right, and center these days. All kinds of people these days are either coming to coaching or interested in coaching. All kinds of businesses are becoming open to the idea of coaching because they're getting it. They're getting that this is not about someone telling people what to do; instead, it is about bringing out the very best in people so that they are using their creativity and their imagination. I see a beautiful upward swing in the coaching profession.

David: And I also think that we're poised for growth because we also do relationship coaching. I think part of the future of coaching is in working with clients with multiple "touch points" in their life. So, one of the places that we both work on is relationship. First and foremost, individual coaching is working on the relationship with your client, discovering how you can be the best you can be when going out into the world, but it's also about your relationship with others. What's that relationship like? Who do you want to be in those relationships?

Cynthia: Most relationships are unconscious, we are on autopilot as we go through our world, and what we're talking about is being conscious and intentional in your life and in your relationships.

***

After Joe and I finished the interview, we continued to be curious how other "A-game Coaches" might answer the same questions, so we contacted neuroscience expert Ann Betz.

Ann Betz, CPCC, PCC, CNTC

Ann is Co-Founder of BEabove Leadership. She is known for her ability to bring cutting-edge theory to life with fun, engaging processes and practical tools. On faculty at the Coaches Training Institute (CTI),

Ann also serves as a consultant to CTI on the neuroscience of coaching. As trainer and coach for both the corporate and non-profit world, designing and leading programs for clients as well as many public school districts and service organizations. A long-time student of consciousness, Ann studied neuroscience on the graduate level at the NeuroLeadership Institute and with Dr. Dan Siegel. Below is Ann's response to the question: What do real coaches do?

Ann: One of the things that real coaches do is we hold the view that human beings are naturally creative and resourceful. That originally comes from the therapist Carl Rogers. It was a new way for therapists to look at people. As coaches, we hold that to mean there are answers within (our clients), and our job as coaches is to help them tap into what's already there. To examine what needs to come into the light, maybe it's just a little whisper of something within that they need to bring out and become more fully aware of.

Here's what the research says: When you work with people in that way, when you ask them rather than tell them what to do, you will find success. We ask them questions like: What's your vision? Where do you see yourself in five years? What's important to you? What values do you want to honor? All of those techniques are what we implement in coach training. When you ask people those questions, the brain is activated in a different way than when you just tell them what to do. When asking people those questions, it activates centers in the brain that are associated with learning, creativity, emotional openness, and interestingly, the part of the brain that is associated with better visual perception. The client can literally "see" things more clearly!

However, often the culture drives us to "fix it" and that's often what people are financially rewarded for, having the right answer and being able to fix it, being the go-to person to wrap everything up. In coaching, we don't do that. We don't hold our client's problems as our own. I'm there as an engaged partner to say, "What do you have going on?" and "How can I find what's already there?" I hope this makes new neural connections and wires in different habits and behaviors so that you fix it or you decide, "I don't care about it and I'm not going to fix it."

Joe: What do you see for the future of coaching?

Ann: Coaching twenty-five years ago was in this innovation space, it was new, it was interesting, it was only with people who were willing to be out there, trying it, getting trained in it and even hiring coaches. When I started coaching, which was fifteen years ago, we were in the early adopter phase so we were starting to get a little more play, there was starting be a little more awareness and a bigger group of people were engaging with it. I think right now coaching is transitioning from early adopter to late adopter.

Joe: So what does late adopter mean?

Ann: In terms of coaching, it used to be that an organization would say, "What's this coaching thing?" What companies are saying now is, "What's our coaching strategy?" or "How are we going to use coaching?" Nike, GE, Google, the US military, and the Peace Corps—we're talking all over the place; this is late adopter territory. People are coming into it, and I think that's exciting. What's happening in the innovation space is the expansion of coaching, expansion into a new field that will include a lot of what we've learned in coaching but will teach us how to be good at things like storytelling, either from our own experience or from wisdom traditions. As a neuroscientist coach, I teach all the time. I teach 75 percent coaching and 25 percent storytelling, teaching people about their brain, sometimes giving advice in a limited way, and I think this is where we are going.

Rick Tamlyn, MCC, CPCC

In our next interview we speak with Rick Tamlyn. He is a Certified Professional Co-Active Coach (CPCC) and a Master Certified Coach (MCC) as designated by the International Coach Federation (ICF). As a Senior Leadership Trainer for The Coaches Training Institute, a world-renowned coach training and leadership development organization, Rick has been instrumental in making leaders of leaders. He has a B.A. in Communications from Hope College in Michigan and an MFA from the University of Connecticut.

In 2001, Rick co-created The Bigger Game: a tool that inspires people from all walks of life to get out of their comfort zones and invent the lives they want. Rick is the author of Play Your Bigger Game: 9 Minutes to Learn, a Lifetime to Live (Hay House, Oct. 2013)

Joe: What do REAL coaches do from your perspective?

Rick: First of all, I was an early adopter. Almost twenty-five years ago, I took a training workshop with the Coaches Training Institute, one of their very first training courses, and I was a huge cynic. Thinking, "this is a fad," "this is going away," "this is sort of silly," yet I had some profound insights into my own learning, to my own psyche, to better understand the concept of where motivation comes from in this workshop. Here I am twenty-five years later translating this and bringing it to the next level. So, I think the good news for folks to know now is that the industry is here to stay.

This is not a fad; this is not a flash in the pan moment, the concept of moving yourself forward and talking to somebody (i.e. a coach) in service of creating a great life is here to stay. A key philosophy that is the reason why coaching works goes like this: Our life moves in the direction of the words that come out of our mouth and the thoughts that are in our head. So, a coach comes along and works with a person, myself included. I have a coach and will have a coach till the end of my life to keep me conscious and awake and clear on what are the words that I'm speaking, mostly in my day to day life, and the thoughts that I'm having.

I think that's the backdrop of why coaching works. We need people to come along and support us and help us get clear about what we want to create with our life and over time, week to week, those conversations start to move our consciousness forward and we begin to create the life we want because we are talking about what we want and we are thinking about what we want. I do believe in the universal principle that words and thoughts create your reality.

So there's the 'behind the scenes' of what I think a coach really does: the profession was born out of a hunger. It was born because we were well-developed in a therapy world, which is a beautiful model. I'm such a fan of it, to be able to take a deep dive into one's psyche, and to understand some of my neuroses and maybe even my psychoses. We all have them. On the other side, way over here, if you put it on a continuum, is consulting. There are therapists and there's consulting, well-developed models, and in the middle was this sort of hybrid.

The word coach came along and said, whom do I talk to about the life I want to create? I don't need to be analyzed (i.e. a therapist) and I don't want to be told what to do (i.e. a consultant). So, this beautiful middle ground appeared called coaching and I think it's an amazing concept. Again, I said it earlier, it's not a one-time "quick fix" model; it is an ongoing conversation, continuing week to week. As I said earlier, I'm going to have a coach for the rest of my life because I want to be conscious, awake, and clear about where I am taking my life. So that's a philosophical viewpoint on why I think coaching is still around and what we really do.

Joe: As we discussed, coaching has been around for twenty-plus years and is still evolving. So what do you think it's evolving into? What's in the space now for coaching?

Rick: Coaching is integrating with the world in technology and creativity and the ability to bring it into my own life (i.e. I can create a movie on my own computer or I can create a song in my house). The ability to create, the concept of creativity is now personalized. These technology companies have brought it into our domain.

So, if that is the backdrop of our world, coaching is moving towards the territory of, "Oh my gosh, as a person I get to manifest and create realities that I never knew I could create." So, we are working with people as coaches asking questions like, "What do you want to create with your life?" which is a different question than "What do you want to create in your life?" "What am I putting out into my world?" versus "What do I want for myself?" I think both are needed in the land of fulfillment, which is about self, what fulfills me.

But for many people, I'm starting to realize as I talk to them, as they create something with their life (i.e. a movie or they are writing a book), they are saying "Oh, it feels so good to create that." I dare say we are in a huge explosive creative phase and if you look at the entrepreneurs and the technology industry, there it is; people are like "What app can I create?" A lot of my clients are talking about what they want to create, so I guess the key words are they're in the "creative phase."

Joe: I'm just going to spin this a little bit, as I'm hearing you saying this, in reference to the coach. Those people who are going into coaching feel this is their opportunity to create the life that they want to live through coaching. They are in their creative space themselves. "How do I want to be as a coach?" "What niche do I want to coach in?"

Rick: Part of that, for a coach, feels so fulfilling on the coach's side as well. When you get off the phone you just want to be able to say, "I loved that conversation" or "I don't know who was coaching whom! They were coaching me, or was I coaching them? I don't know but I want more of those conversations!" and it's that richness of conversation rather than your "fixing a problem" over there in a person and then hanging up the phone and we're done. So, it's really about the kind of conversation you want to be having.

I think a coach needs to be asking that. So, the coach gets to decide, "What's the conversation that I want to be having?" and that's a key component to attracting clients. The coach has to decide, "What do I love talking about with my clients?" Then, the rest of the world responds, "This coach is looking for that conversation; good, I'll send people in that direction." I've seen it happen over and over again.

The law of attraction works. What I think what we are talking about, and what I think coaching is moving toward, is having people realize that they are a part of the world. We're all a part of this. It's not happening to me, and I'm not completely responsible to it, meaning my world. But we're always co-creating it, always, always, always. That can be a fairly advanced concept because people bounce through life with their circumstances and they're affecting, if you will, their circumstances.

I think a coach comes along, and this is a conversation I'm having a lot with my clients, to raise the awareness, to help them realize,

"Okay, wait a minute, these circumstances are happening…how do I want to interact with these circumstances?" is the first question. But the second question, which is a little deeper and a little further out on the edge is, "What was my part in creating that circumstance?" Now sometimes that's a difficult moment, like how could that be, for somebody who is ill, you know, "How did I create that?" It's a fairly advanced question and there's not a singular answer but it does move the bar up to say, "I am a part of this world, I am not an effect of this world, I am co-creating with it."

Is Coaching Right for You?

Coaching is for those who want a deeper understanding of who they really are; for those who are ready to connect with their life and business on an entirely new level. If you don't know what you want, that is okay. Bring that question with you to your coaching session. Coaching is for those interested in possibilities. It is transformational space you can create for yourself to find out your next big thing. You know that regardless of what has happened to you in the past, every moment can be a new day and every breath you take is a chance for you to start in a new direction.

> *Begin with the end in mind.*
> *-Stephen Covey*

Imagine sometime in the future, your friends and loved ones are gathered at your funeral. As you hover over this time and place, you see people you didn't even know who cared for you deeply. They are taking time to honor you and the good that you brought into the world. Take a moment now and imagine who is there and what might they be saying about you?

My husband and I attended a retreat called "The Jangle" by Thomas (Peters) Qafzezi and Lucetta Zaytoun, who I mentioned earlier. They led us through aforementioned meditation which was a transformational turning point for me. I envisioned people saying that

I gave them hope. That day it became clear to me that my life purpose is "to inspire a life well-lived."

Now, as a leader, this gave me what people call my "why," by seriously thinking about what I want my last Transformation on this earth to look like. Maybe you have an idea of what that is for you and you're afraid to admit it. Maybe you're afraid that somehow your life as you know it today will be over and you're not quite sure what life will be like for you once you embrace what you really stand for in this world. I mention that because I felt that way at one time. **I didn't want to take the time to answer deep questions as if by not answering them it would buy me more time on the earth to figure it out.**

Once I became clear of what I wanted people to say at my funeral, the leadership stake for my business became self-evident and easy for me to convey to others. Like I said earlier, one of my stakes as a leader is: "When we are fulfilled at work, we are happier at home; when we are happier at home, our world is a better place." The clarity and conviction of that message helped my business take off. Being able to simply begin with the end in mind will result in true alignment of your personal vision and purpose with your business goals. Now it's time to make this real for you.

Your Transformation Strategy

1. What is important to you about your life and legacy as a leader?

2. Take a moment now and reflect on the main impact you want to have on others throughout your life. What is it?

3. Why did you choose your profession? What do you want people to most remember about you?

4. How much time do you spend actually doing the things you want to be remembered for?

5. What is your Leadership Stake? (What do you believe and what is your anticipated outcome based on that belief?)

Below is a transcript from a conversation I recently had with one of my leadership clients, Patrick. Initially, when he signed up for my leadership program months ago, he knew he wasn't ready to leave his franchise AND at the same time he wanted:

- A "safe space" to go where he could hear himself think

- To be around other leaders he respected and enjoyed

- To maximize his time and money by listening to others who have been where he is going

- To more clearly identify his brand as a leader

- One place where he could access all the business, career and leadership tools he needed

- Get support for his Transition Plan.

Through our program he's discovering new emerging opportunities within the organization that didn't appear before. So I asked him, "What have you gained from our program so far?"

Patrick answered, "Your program has inspired me to go with what I know I need, and to not compromise on the quality of people that I select. As a result, I've developed a profile for the kind of people I want to work with in my company; people who have certain skill sets and have both the willingness and ability to go where we need to be."

"I notice that when I invest in my own personal leadership development, my business margins jump, for the better. Right now, my chain is performing in the top 20% in at least 80% of our corporate measures. On the profit end, over the past decade, we have consistently performed within the top 5%-10% of the chain; however, over the past few months we have elevated and now we are in the top 1%!"

"My finance department reviewed my $4M P&L (Profit and Loss statement) and could only find opportunities to save on our phone bill, which is about $5k a year. I've always invested in my development, but this program has given me a laser focus. The best way I can describe it is being on a mountaintop and the higher I get (in my own personal and professional development), the more I can see other hills and mountains (opportunities) that I never knew existed."

I replied, Wow! I am so impressed with you and your leaders. These numbers are amazing and truly about your leadership and your Crew. What never ceases to amaze me is the fact that when you made a commitment to your own development, so many things fell into place for you and those around you.

In conclusion, I'll leave you with this: one simple way you as Business Leader can start preparing for Transformation to occur is to spend more time "working ON the business" versus "IN the business." This means taking a step back and looking at your business strategy and leadership. The goal is to comfortably delegate work to someone you trust, AND someone who admits their mistakes, AND can work IN the business for you when you are not around. Once this power is given, be very careful in taking it back!

I've seen so many Business Leaders come into the middle of a project and disrupt their people by giving directions that conflict with those given by the assigned leader. This not only pulls the rug out from under the leader on the ground, it also confuses the team members as to who is really in charge of the project. Remember to keep the end in mind, which is building leaders and being present with them when they fail. Of course, you need to know your limits, but how important is that failure versus living your legacy?

"T" is for Transition Plan

Everyone has been made for some particular work, and the desire for that work has been put in every heart.
-Rumi

Today, most people can expect to have multiple employers and careers over their lifetime, AND if you're an entrepreneur you probably already have several businesses at one time, too. Many of us start in one career and learn what we need to and then become ready to start something much more meaningful and sustainable. So it's important to think about having a Transition Plan.

Let me give you a real-life example as to why having a Transition Plan is so important. My client, Steve, built an international non-profit organization from the ground up. The organization empowers children to protect themselves and escape rape and abduction. As he enters a new phase in his life, he wants his organization to continue beyond his years. How does he transition to becoming a spokesperson and find someone with the same passion, dedication and knowledge to sustain his vision? One way you can start thinking about what you need versus what your business or your organization needs is by creating a strategy model.

Strategy Model

Typically, a strategy model allows leaders to tell their own strategic story:

- What are we trying to accomplish?

- What gaps will need to be solved?

- How will we get where we want to be?

As you can see, this strategy model centers around a Motivated Workforce (key to sustaining an organizational vision). It beautifully depicts people as central to all else (opportunities, goals, problems etc.) This model can be used for you to initiate goal setting and planning discussions with other leaders. It is one of my favorite models to start business conversations with because it helps Business Leaders understand what milestones need to be discussed. Finally, notice that Career Development is a primary goal and Talent Effectiveness is a Success Measure. We'll talk more about goals in the next section.

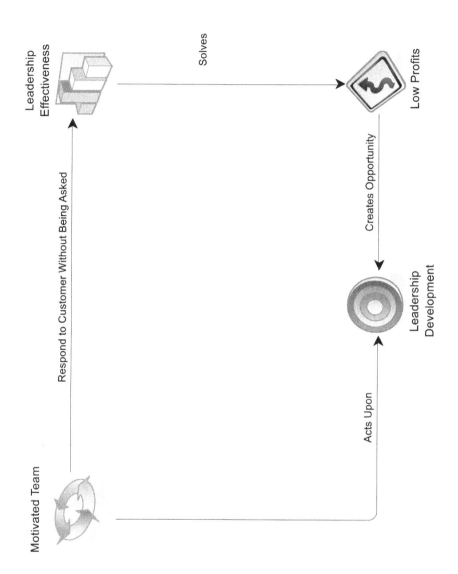

Goal Model

Successful Business Leaders and entrepreneurs often start out with interconnected short, intermediate and long-term goals. As in life, operating a business is a journey toward some destination. Some of us know where we want to end up, but far too many have no idea where they are headed in life and are at the mercy of "blowing in the wind" and cursing the outcome.

In many cases, an entrepreneur will start a business with the intention of never selling it. Others want to build their business up and sell it off once the business has become successful. (Sometimes just a good idea taken to the next step of implementation can trigger a quick sale!) Others build a business for the long-term benefit to themselves, their family, stockholders, employees and even communities.

I like to refer to having a Transition Plan as similar to navigating over long distances; you are more likely to arrive at your destination in the least amount of time and with the least hassles if you know where you are going and how to get there. Have you ever been on a boat at sea? You start to feel queasy until some sea-savvy person tells you to "keep your eyes on a point on the horizon."

If you don't have some sort of long-term goal to keep your eye on during your business-oriented journey, you can get lost. Indeed, today, even some of the largest and most well-known businesses are "re-inventing" themselves. Whether you are working within an existing company or are a Business Owner, successful Business Leaders know when to move on; in short, they know when to head for the exit. This is where your intuition, or your Leader Within, comes into play.

Again, whether you are a leader of a small or large organization, you will want to establish strong goals and success measures. Here is an example of the balanced score card goals (customer, employee, financial and process goals) and related measures of success that are beneficial when considering your Transition Plan.

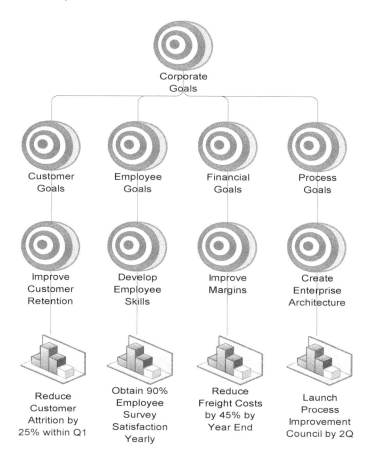

Whether you're a Business Owner, or a Business Leader staying within an organization, it's never too late to consider how you want to transition your involvement. To support you with this decision, consider the following:

"Passing the Baton"

This is a tricky undertaking as the personalities, experiences and motivations of the Business Leader and the next generation can be very different. Further, we don't always get to choose who we want to transition our responsibilities to. However, transitioning the business to employees or family members is an excellent way for company leaders to move to their next big thing like retiring (whatever that means these days) so that they can continue receiving income and benefits from ongoing profits.

"Build and Flip"

Most young entrepreneurs see a Transition Plan as building a business to expand products or services to various markets and selling-off divisions and accumulating wealth as they liquidate the old and develop the new.

"Hitting the Homerun"

Becoming a public company is generally thought of as the "big payoff," as public investors pour in money, making all founding shareholders millionaires (or billionaires) overnight. Business Nirvana.

"Retiring"

Retiring is different for everyone. Primarily it is when we as leaders establish a certain lifestyle and then accumulate enough income to cover all lifestyle expenses, no matter if we "work" or not. The thing to remember is, once all toys, assets and risks are hedged, then what?

Whatever your Transition Plan, all Business Leaders need to consider their transition away from a company, project or initiative as an anchor point for the planned business evolution, to become a destination point. A business is an asset for producing wealth for its ownership and an income for its employees. It produces wealth by accumulating profits that can be used to build up equity in the business or to purchase other investments to produce even more wealth. Moreover, taxes from profits and employee wages are the financial underpinnings of all governments.

Maybe you've seen the old bumper sticker on some humongous and expensive-looking RV being driven by a couple of white-haired senior citizens as it passes by: "He who dies with the most toys, wins."

While rather flippant, unfortunately, this may be the shallow mindset that can drive us.

What happens to many good leaders is they become numb by the demands of their business and responsibilities. This is why it's so important to learn how to develop other leaders to share in your vision. **The sad truth is that too many Business Leaders become so attached to their role that they forget *who* they are and *what* they want.** Their life starts and ends with the business. Their world has shrunk to the size of their rather trivial daily business concerns.

When we talk about a Transition Plan, we help focus on our relationship to the business. Being successful in business is a means to an end, and what is that end? By having a destination, we can establish milestones along the journey. Those become both short and intermediate goals that work best when we celebrate our failures and successes along the way.

Bottom-line: As a Business Leader, you need to take time to pause and refresh by setting short celebratory milestones along the way. However, it should not only be business milestones that are measured. As a leader with a strong potential influence, if you want to be truly satisfied as you move along in your career, you may also want a development plan that includes helping your community. Identify those areas in which you as a person need to improve and make action plans for those intangibles that will link your success in business with your success as a person.

At the end of your Transition Plan, "your personal intangible assets" will have much more value to you than your net worth. The first step is to be 99.99% committed to having your work-life enhance your lifestyle and the rest will fall into place. You don't need to know all the answers and you don't have to go it alone. Just take one step at a time; one minute at a time. If you can authentically work every day to create Alignment, surround yourself with the right Crew, and always look towards your Transformation Strategy and Transition Plan, you will **ACTT** on attaining success in your personal and professional life as you INSPIRE others to follow in your footsteps. This could be your legacy. Your greatest triumph.

If you decide to follow the **ACTT Blueprint** I mention in this chapter, it's best to inform your Crew to help maximize the time spent on developing a business and work life you want to create. In fact, if you can plan for your transition while still bringing in the bacon, it can help calm those feelings of urgency that make you want to move on right now rather than keeping your frustrations and ambitions contained until the time is right.

If you have trouble starting your ACTT Blueprint, remember, most leaders don't even get started because we subcontract our Captain role to other people, places or things. We get stuck caught between two competing values. We think to ourselves, "I can't quit my job! I need it." Or "I am used to a certain standard of living." The truth is you never know when your job will quit you; it's usually wise to choose when you leave for greener pastures. Also, make a graceful transition and don't burn bridges as your ex-employer may become a customer in the future.

Whether you work for a large corporation or you work for yourself, you will one day inevitably find yourself doing something other than what you are doing now. Perhaps you work for someone else and you are seeing some things in the workplace that don't align with your values. You might be thinking, "How much more of this can I tolerate?" Whether you decide to switch departments, get a promotion or start your own business, you—like everyone else—need a Transition Plan. If you don't plan your own transition, someone else or some event will create one for you.

Your Transition Plan

So let's make this real for you:

- What is your Transition Plan for your current career or business?
  - Passing the baton to another leader or family member?

- o Retiring (whatever that means these days!)?

- o Getting promoted?

- o Building a business and then liquidating it?

- o Hitting a home run and going public with your company?

- o Other ideas?

- How many of your written goals align with your Transition Plan? Once you know your end game, then you can execute your plan.

- What one major milestone will you complete this month? Next month? This quarter? By the end of this year?

Real ACTT Leaders Transition from Ordinary to Extraordinary

To inspire you, the following **ACTT** leadership examples are real events lived by people just like YOU.

Ray is a proponent of the **ACTT Blueprint**. In other words, he has Aligned values, and is committed to his priorities. He is a C-level executive who "discovered" his true desires and abilities while helping his Crew solve some serious problems. His Crew took the company's vision and goals and crafted a solution initiative based on the alignment of the company's values. His case was convincing as it was practical, so his board of directors approved Ray's new initiative, saving his company millions of dollars every year. The transformational thrill of helping the company as well as understanding how to analyze problems and aligning solutions led Ray to transitioning to a more fulfilling career as a consultant with his company, rather than just punching the time clock as an employee.

I'd like to tell you another short story. The profile of a real, live **ACTT** Leader. I have her permission to share these details; however, she asked that I keep her name confidential, and I respect that.

This leader is a very successful C-level executive in a company that has grown 10x over the last 10 years. As the company has grown, now to billions of dollars in sales, the culture has gradually shifted from one of entrepreneurial energy to a "growth and income" model. "Smart decisions" have replaced intuition and risk-taking, AND shareholder value is replacing sustainability. She is proud of the company that she helped build, yet wants to exercise her creative and entrepreneurial spirit. The owners of her company might not approve of a focus outside of the company core.

How does she continue in her current position and set herself up for a great entrepreneurial adventure? Through the **ACTT** approach, she examined her interactions in her current position and determined how to shift her actions to be consistent with her _A_lignment of personal values. "Live now, instead of simply surviving." As a result, her credibility at the company has continued to grow as she acts from her powerful Leader Within. **Also, she committed time to her _T_rans-formation Strategy and her _C_rew, her mastermind group who can spring into action when called upon.**

Last, she has determined her _T_ransition to launch her next creation. Within a few months, she expects that her company will be sold, and she could potentially make millions in options. In the meantime, she continues to prepare for the next adventure as an author. Ready to hear more from **ACTT** Leaders? Keep reading.

CEO of MorningCoach.com, JB Glossinger's Story

JB Glossinger is the founder of MorningCoach.com, and inspires millions each day with energizing and inspiring messages. JB's podcasts have consistently been at the top of the charts for iTunes, beating Oprah and other celebrities with his inspirational messages. JB is a motivational speaker, author, coach and consultant. And, as told by his tongue-in-cheek words, is also a "modern day archeologist bringing esoteric wisdom to the masses." **He will blow you away with his passion and common sense advice on creating the life of your dreams.** Here is my interview with him in December 2015.

Nina: Thanks so much for spending some time with me today. A lot of people ask me how I got started, so I just want to ask you to share a little about your background and what made you leave corporate and start out on your own.

JB: Oh, yes, I was miserable coming into work, but let me take a step back. I started off in sales and built a pretty good reputation in aviation that eventually led to a position on the board of directors for a small company where I ran the division for the company. I thought I'd found my dream. You know, I got a MBA, I went up the corporate ladder, I was making all this money, but I was miserable. Literally, I would wait till Thursday to get to Friday, but then I would start drinking Friday night. On Saturday and Sunday, I would have a hangover, and then I would feel good enough to go back Monday and travel or do what I needed to do. Couldn't realize why I felt like my life sucked. *This blows; I am living the dream,* I would think. I remember this Wednesday night after sitting in traffic, coming home, thinking, *look, you're living the dream, you should appreciate this. You got the great house, you got a great car, you got the company car, you got everything you need,* and I was just miserable. One day I did a values assessment on myself to figure out what was really important and what my number-one value, above everything, was. I know this is weird for a lot of people because spirituality and family is number one, but my number one value is freedom, and I realized that sitting in that office or travelling around the world working for somebody else was not going to make me happy. That is why I was self-medicating as much as I was every weekend; I was actually crumbling inside. That is why I had to leave corporate.

Nina: Wow, I'm so glad you did because you affect hundreds of thousands of people's lives every day; you bring so much inspiration into the world.

JB: Well, we try. When I was gonna make the move, my roommate said no, he told me, JB, nobody will listen to you. I waited a year and half because I listened to him. He said, you've got a great career. People around me who loved me the most were telling me, "You're crazy, don't leave, you've built this great career, why would you ever leave?" Sometimes those who love you can actually harm you with their love. You gotta be cautious of that.

Nina: Yes, we were talking about how important other people are around you and how important it is to have a Crew and good mastermind group. So thanks for sharing that. It's good to know, especially if it works for everybody.

JB: You've gotta have the right people around you; that's one of the secrets (to success), making sure you have the right people in your corner.

Nina: Lots of people are still in corporate and they're not so sure they have a desire to leave. They want this freedom but they're not sure how to do it without destroying their life, you know, losing financial stability. What would you say to them?

JB: I understand. I destroyed my stability when I did it. I didn't use what I call intelligent life design, which is using your brain, being smart about it, and structuring something on the side until you can leave. Anybody can do that in the world today with the internet. We're showing that in this interview. There are so many things you can do today. So keep your job, there is nothing wrong with that, and focus on building something on the side. You can build monster businesses between eight at night and midnight, that is four hours a night, or if you've got children, nine at night till midnight or 10 at night till one. Get up an hour early. So it's the motivation you need in order to have that happen. You don't ever want to leave your business or income. You wanna start generating something on the side so you can see, *hey, this is gonna work,* then you can make that choice one day; *okay, I have enough money, let's make the decision to blow. Let's go do this.*

Nina: I love that because what I hear you saying is stay committed to your dreams, even if it takes a while, just keep doing whatever you need to do, and then just do it, make it happen.

JB: Yes, it's taken me eight years. The first five years I lost my house when I left and I didn't use that intelligent life design. I just left and my career failed; it was really ugly, but we survived. After five years we started becoming a little profitable and after seven years' things got a lot better. Now we are coming into our ten-year mark and things are amazing. So it's like an elegy, a 10-year overnight success. So yes, you gotta persist in running this thing that you are after. But if I had to do it all over again, no, I would have kept the job and put a little more on the side so I didn't have to go through the financial strain I did.

Nina: It's not as simple as, "Hey, we reached success." What many don't realize is there are ups and downs along the way and it is not always a straight shot into success.

JB: No. Some people hit it and things work for them, but failure is all part of the process; failure leads to learning, which leads to success. You gotta go through that to grow because ultimately the reason that you may not be successful right out of the gate is because you have to change. You have to grow; you have to become that entrepreneur. In corporate it is very simple: you go to work, you do what you need to do, and you get a paycheck. As soon as you step out of that, that paycheck is not coming in. So you've got to change the way you think, the way you approach your life, the way you approach your business; everything changes. I am famous now for golfing every day. I am famous for not having a calendar or keeping appointments, it's not what I do. The truth is that I get more done because of the way I think now and the ability to put systems in place. I had to learn how to do that.

Nina: You said earlier your day flows and you always make time for fun. It sounds like that's your everyday practice.

JB: Yes, I'm allergic to work. I'm lazy and I just don't want to work. It's not fun to me. This is fun to me so I don't consider it work. There are just a few times when I work, like when the books are coming back from an edit, like the fifth edit. *I gotta get this done*, so okay, that's work. I try to do that in the morning. Do whatever I hate first thing in the morning and then that's out of the way, so now I can do the fun stuff. Which is internet marketing and funnels; to me that's fun, so I don't consider that work.

Nina: I love your energy because a lot of people think, *oh my gosh, I'm gonna spend time doing that?* But when you love something, you get more energy to do it, and that is so evident in the way you are conducting your life right now.

JB: Exactly. It's just awesome when you do what you love; the energy will come, and it comes from when you start to get into the flow. That's metaphysical, so we won't go there today. I want everybody to find that passion because that's what drives you and part of intelligent life design is not only doing something on the side but doing something you really love, because that is the true secret to success.

Nina: If people want to find out more about you and your book where do they go or what should they do?

JB: MorningCoach.com is easy to find. I also have books on Amazon.

Nina: Thank you so much for taking time out of your day to meet with me and thank you for sharing your wisdom with us. I appreciate you.

JB: No problem, it's great to be here. Let's keep rocking it out there.

Eric Yuan CEO of Zoom Story

Here is another story from Eric Yuan who is a Happiness Expert, CEO and Founder of Zoom Communication, Inc. His amazing video application brings happiness to millions with personal connections each week! He spent 14 Years at Cisco/Webex, as Corporate Vice President of Engineering prior to starting at Zoom. He understands what it's like to work as a Business Leader within a large corporation and then start his own business.

Nina: Thank you for joining me today. Eric, what happened that pushed you over the edge to leave Cisco and start Zoom.us?

Eric: This boils down to how to pursue happiness. Because Cisco is a bigger company, I wanted to create a service to make the world a better place and to empower others to enjoy life using our solutions. That is my dream. And because of that, I left the big company and created a startup. Instead of sitting idle, I built a positive and proactive solution that millions of people enjoy using. So that's how I pursue happiness.

Nina: Wow, that's powerful. So as you are pursuing your own happiness, you are inspiring the happiness of others.

Eric: Absolutely, yes.

Nina: How long did it take you to act on your decision to leave Cisco?

Eric: It was not an easy decision because Cisco is a great company. However, I did not want to have regrets. I think those startup companies are really driving the economy forward. I decided if I did not work for a startup company, I would not have the speed necessary to build an innovative solutions company. That is why a startup company is probably the best vehicle for me to pursue happiness.

Nina: It sounds like starting up a company isn't for everyone, but for you, that's what you had to do; there was no way around it.

Eric: Yeah.

Nina: If you were to advise young entrepreneurs on how they can keep their financial stability and still pursue their dreams, what tips would you give them?

Eric: First of all, you've got to work hard, even if you think you are very smart. There is no other way to be successful. Secondly, you've got to be very patient. Along the way you need to learn new things every day. Work hard, learn new things and be patient, and as you go down the road you will be successful. You need to understand your dream to ensure you are happy. As you mentioned earlier, if you are not happy at work, then you cannot be happy at home and vice versa.

Nina: It sounds like what got you where you are today by being patient. In order to be patient it sounds like you had to sort through some disappointment and maybe some criticism. You just kept going and your tenacity and your commitment to your happiness kept you going. Is that about right?

Eric: Yes.

Nina: Wow, that's inspiring. Eric, who is in your Crew? We talk about Crew here in BusinessCoachingOnDemand.com, that's the people who are committed to your success 99.99%. These would include coaches, mentors, or partners. So who is in your Crew?

Eric: That is a great question. First of all, if you're a leader you've got to have a dream. You've got to have your own vision, and you need to find those team members who share the same vision, that share the same philosophies. Those who value work, patience, pursuing happiness, if you can find those team members, you'll have your Crew.

Nina: What's the number one thing that you want all of your employees to know?

Eric: How to deliver happiness to our customers. That is the number-one most important thing.

Nina: Eric, I'm always so impressed with the way your technology sales and support team treats me. Even when I had the free service they were still treating me the same as anyone else. I have to say, as a Business Owner and entrepreneur, to have the strong technology support that we can call anytime is just so meaningful. Thank you for pursuing your dream and inspiring others.

Eric: You are welcome. Thank you for having me.

I hope that these stories have inspired you. Remember, don't compare your backyard to someone's front yard. Meaning we are all in different phases of our journey. The first step to take is simply doing one thing every day to fulfill your dream career. To get you started, you can use the following Business Mastery Assessment. This will help you complete the worksheet that follows it (*The ACTT Blueprint for Leaders and Entrepreneurs*). Or if you're rebellious like me, just skip to the second worksheet below. They work in conjunction with one another so the order doesn't matter. What does matter is that you're creating forward, focused movement toward your legacy as a leader.

Business Mastery Assessment

Take a look at these key questions and draft your answers. This is a working document. Visit this document each month to make changes and celebrate your successes.

The first step in getting your ACTT together is to know where you are right now. We will use this baseline to develop your ACTT Blueprint. **Read the definition and key questions for each area. Rate yourself.** Don't be too disappointed if you discover low numbers, this is the beginning and we build from here! *Your Name_____ Date_____*

How Aligned are you?		*Rank* *1-10* *(10 is highest)*
*Top Values These are the top values that you hold dear in both your personal and professional work life.	To what extent do your actions relate to the values you affirm to be important in both your personal and professional work life?	
*Life Purpose This is your bigger picture, what you are up to in this world, your impact, your legacy. Sometimes it's a metaphor such as "I am the bridge connecting people home."	To what extent are you living your life purpose daily? To what extent does your work life reflect your life purpose?	
Vision This is how you want life to be like both at work and at home. This is who and how you want to be AND by when.	Think about your vision for your business and work life, how closely does your reality reflect your vision?	

Edge These are the talents and skills that set you apart and help your business do what it does best. It is what makes you a unique business leader.	If you are clear on your edge, to what extent are you using your edge to your advantage?	
Mission This is how you will obtain your vision, it's the actions you will take to create the world you want.	To what extent does your business contribute to your vision of the world? How well does the mission for your business align with your life's purpose?	
Stump Speech Statement This is your pitch: "I help (client/group of clients) (how you fill their gaps) so that (your impact)." Examples: *"I provide Business Leaders in transition practical tools and transformational experiences needed for a meaningful AND prosperous work life."* Or *"I help Medical Professionals unleash their potential so that they can positively impact their patients and their community."*	How developed is your stump speech regarding the work you want to be doing now? How clearly can you articulate to whom you aim your services? How clearly can you describe what you deliver and its impact or benefit?	
	Sub Total	
Alignment Assessment	**Divide your subtotal by 6 and record that number below.**	
	How Aligned are you?	

Who is on your Crew?		Rank 1-10 (10 is highest)
Crew Members These are the relationships that are key to your professional and personal success. These are your mentors, coaches, Life and Business partners, etc. Your crew cheers you on, inspires you and acts as a resource when you need assistance. They can be personal connections, or authors, speakers, notable figures that you admire and from whom you learn and gather support.	How robust is your crew? How connected do you feel to your crew? How connected are you to professionals who can support you?	
Your Ideal Client(s) Your ideal Client(s) are those who you want to most positively impact. You need to know the characteristics of your ideal Client to serve them.	How clearly can you identify the characteristics of your ideal Client(s)? How well does your daily work flow serve your ideal Client(s)? What are the demographics of your Clients? How will you get in front of them? Where do they go? What do they do? What are neighboring (like) industries that serve them?	
Ideal Crew List additional Crew members that you need to attract your Ideal Clients.	How clearly developed is your Ideal Crew?	

Your Leadership SuperPowers List your Leadership SuperPowers here (visit www.NinaSegura.com/SuperPowers). Also, include what you know about your work style, work preferences and appropriate business model for your entrepreneur style if applicable e.g. Myers Briggs Type, DiSC, Wealth Dynamics assessments etc.	How closely aligned is the work you are doing with your Leadership SuperPowers?	
	Sub Total	
Crew Assessment	**Divide your subtotal by 4 and record that number below.**	
	How robust is your Crew?	

What is your Transformation Strategy?		*Rank* *1-10* *(10 is highest)*
Your Beliefs These are the messages you tell yourself that help or hinder your mission. Examples: I am enough. I have enough time for everything. I can make a good living and still have time for fun. I deserve to be successful. I can start my day all over again at any time.	To what extent are your beliefs supporting you to get what you deserve?	

Transformational Actions	To what extent do you create	
These are the actions you take to support your vision becoming reality. It's what you do on a consistent basis so that you have the time and resources to be who you want to be. Examples: *exercise daily, meet coach weekly, attend mastermind group semi-monthly, etc.*	space on a consistent basis so that you have the time and resources to be who you want? To do what you want to do?	
Customer Life Cycle Strategy	How well-defined is your customer life cycle strategy? How robust are your ongoing mechanisms for outreach and loyalty and customer advocacy?	
This is how your customers are made aware of your product/services. It's what you do to convince them to purchase and to stay loyal to you.		
Leadership Stake	How clear are you about your work life beliefs?	
This is what you believe about the work you do. It's the impact you want to have.

Example 1: *When people are fulfilled at work, they are happier at home.*

Example 2: *We are most effective as leaders when we lean in fully to the resources of our Crew.* | How clear are you about the impact your work life is having or will have? | |
| **Sales Strategy** | Do you know what sales strategy works best with your SuperPowers as a leader? How close to implementing this strategy are you? | |
| If you are a leader you need to know how to sell your ideas, products and or services.

Include how you're selling or going to sell based on your SuperPowers. | | |

	Sub Total	
Transformation Assessment	**Divide your subtotal by 5 and record that number below.**	
	How defined is your Transformation Strategy?	

What is your Transition Plan?		*Rank* *1-10* *(10 is highest)*
Transition Actions This is either how you will move into or out of where you are (pass the baton –transition my role to someone else, franchise my business, sell my IP etc.) It includes timelines for the financial and emotional aspects and any applicable processes e.g. reflecting, gathering information, requesting recommendations, updating your online presence, joining professional organizations, resignation etc.	How developed is your transition plan? How clear are you on the factors that need to be analyzed for transition? How clear is your timeline?	
Financials This includes the planning for both future passive and active incomes.	How clearly can you articulate your income, revenue & budget goals (before, during & after your transition)?	

Initiatives These are the top three to five initiatives you need to do to advance your business, achieve your vision.	How clearly articulated are your top three to five initiatives? How close are you to being able to achieve them?	
Development This includes the assignments and next steps that will help you develop most effectively. It's also knowing the strengths upon which you can build.	How clearly can you identify developmental tasks for yourself? How clear are you on your own strengths? Areas for growth?	
Market Landscape This is knowing how what happens in the market will impact you. It includes being aware of trends, risks and opportunities.	How aware of your market landscape are you? How friendly is the landscape to your business model?	
Performance Measures & Metrics These are the specific, measurable results that define success in your business.	How closely connected are your success measures with what you need to achieve TODAY to the results you need in the long run?	
	Sub Total	
Transition Assessment for Business Leaders.	**Divide your subtotal by 6 and record that number below for <u>Business Leaders.</u>**	
	How well-developed is your Transition Plan?	

The Following Question is for _Business Owners_ Only.		Rank 1-10 (10 is highest)
Revenue Models (Business Owners Only)	How closely connected are you with the business model that will produce the most significant monetary results.	
	Sub Total	
Transition Assessment for Business Owners.	**Divide your subtotal by 7 and record that number below for Business Owners.**	
	How well-developed is your Transition Plan?	

ACTT Blueprint Business Mastery Assessment Totals

Copy your ratings from each section.	
How _A_ligned are you?	
Who is on your _C_rew?	
What is your _T_ransformation Plan?	
What is your _T_ransition Plan?	

Helpful Hints:

***As you continue to evolve the above Business Mastery Assessment transfer your information to the below *ACTT BLUEPRINT FOR LEADERS AND ENTREPRENUERS*. Review your **ACTT BLUEPRINT** WITH YOUR CREW MONTHLY.

**To get an on-line, downloadable copy of the Business Mastery Assessment and make it your own, go to www.NinaSegura.com/bonus.

Every Day is Friday ACTT Blueprint for Leaders and Entrepreneurs! Worksheet

ACTT on Every Day being a Friday by using this Blueprint.

The ACTT Blueprint for Leaders will help reveal the fastest path to fulfillment AND prosperity!

Your Name_____ Date _____

How Aligned are you?

My Top Values:	
My Life Purpose:	
Vision:	
Edge:	
Mission:	
Stump Speech Statement:	

Who is on your Crew?

My Crew:	

My Ideal Client(s):	
My Ideal Crew (include missing roles):	
*My Leadership SuperPowers:	

What is your Transformation Strategy?

My Beliefs:	
I commit to these actions ...	
My Customer Life Cycle Strategy?	
*My Stake: A Stake is your belief and the outcome based on that belief.	
Sales Strategy:	

What is your Transition Plan?

Every Business Leader needs a transition plan (e.g. Pass the Baton to another person, Franchise my business, etc.)	
Financials (including your financial goals):	

One Major Milestone I will Accomplish Monthly based on initiatives and development items):	Key Habits:	Measures of Success:
1. 2. 3. 4. 5. 6. 7. 8. 9. 10. 11. 12.		

My Top 5 Priority Actions in the Next 90 Days:	Due:	Notes:

How I will Celebrate:	
How I will Recalibrate: How will you feel about yourself when you make mistakes? E.g. Be gentle with yourself and call someone supportive, etc.	

If you want to be a great Business Leader, you need to **ACTT**! First, gain Alignment; second, engage your Crew; third, understand your Transformation Strategy; and finally, create a Transition Plan!

Helpful Hints:

- When you have completed this put it in a place where you can see it every day. Consider updating it once a month at minimum.

- Celebrate small successes along the way.

- This is a work in progress. Mistakes will be made!

- Written goals have a greater chance of being accomplished.

- Kick it up a notch by sharing your **ACTT** plan with as many people as possible.

- ***Visit** www.NinaSegura.com/SuperPowers

CHAPTER FOUR
SUPER LEADERSHIP

Take a moment now and imagine your perfect day. You wake up and... What happens? Where are you? Who are you talking to? How are they responding to you? How do you feel as you imagine this day? Or have you forgotten how to let yourself dream? I hope not. When you have a good idea of your vision, your next step is to share your vision with your Crew around you.

The interesting thing here is that EVERYONE IS A LEADER by the very nature of the fact that when we enter a room, we impact those in our surroundings. Some of us are more skillful leaders than others in creating a positive impact. However skilled we may be at leadership, all of us will have intended and unintended impacts from the choices we make. You may be a good fit for entrepreneurship, or you may be happy working as a leader in another capacity; regardless of what role you play, here are a few Super Leader Essentials.

Super Leader Essentials

If you're reading this book you probably want your team to be appropriately self-directed and high performing so that you can rely on them always. As a leader, you have spent so much time and money to be where you are today. You have business targets that need to be met AND you need your team to help get you there. Oftentimes, you need to run a team and you're left without much guidance or direction on how to build a successful team—what we call a Super Team.

These days, leaders such as yourself are faced with the harsh reality that if things don't change, their top performers will leave and then all the pressure will be on those remaining to have the answers and resolve conflicts. I know you don't want to be put on your boss's (or your BOD) watch list and you definitely don't want Human Resources to be worried about liability issues under your umbrella. There's a huge misconception that because we are educated leaders, we should know how to lead teams (and even more challenging, virtual teams), and that is just not true. So I'd like to share with you keys to being a Super Leader.

Listen to Your Intuition

The first thing that Super Leaders do is tap into their intuition like never before (think California gold rush in the 1850s). Your intuition (Leader Within) is gold. For those of you that need all the facts before making a decision, I completely get it. As a certified Six Sigma Black Belt (statistical process improvement methodology), I understand how important 99.99% is! However, when you are a Super Leader, your team needs you to tap in to your intuition. It will help you to know when to pick up the phone and have a conversation or send that email, or neither. Intuition often feels the same as our Leader Within and is something we are all born with and we can learn to develop.

Vulnerability Brings Safety and Connection

Secondly, Super Leaders are **appropriately vulnerable**. You as the leader need to provide the foundation of trust for the team. The best way to do that is to be vulnerable when necessary. One way you can do this is to simply ask your team to bring a meaningful photo with them to the next meeting. Team members can share stories about something meaningful for them outside of work. This can even be done if you are meeting virtually. Maybe it will be a photo of their beloved pet or one of their cute kids—you may have more in common than you think. Maybe they will introduce you to a new vacation spot! The more you get your team to share something vulnerably appropriate, the less you will have to manage them.

Entrepreneurial Thinking

Finally, the most important thing that Super Leaders do is they think like entrepreneurs AND they get their teams to think collectively and independently like Business Owners, too. This has nothing to do with whether you are currently a Business Owner! Every successful entrepreneur learned to build their business around their strengths, or as we are calling them, SuperPowers. So it's important that you know your team's SuperPowers.

Working within Fortune 100 companies most of my adult life, I have found they all have one goal in common: to keep the profits high and the expenses low. Most of them want to positively impact their community and have a strong base of sustainability. However, when companies get too large, they lose the entrepreneurial and team thinking that got them there in the first place.

Learning how to think like an entrepreneur, even if you are a corporate employee, is very beneficial for your career. Why? Most entrepreneurs will take calculated risks in service to their customers and manage change by establishing a vision and maintaining flexibility when things don't go as planned. When that doesn't agree with the current corporate model, the thought behind the behavior is, "It's better to ask for forgiveness than permission." Further, entrepreneurs are not afraid to wear any "hat" needed to get things done. The entrepreneurs that built businesses from the ground up also know what it is like to do work with very little resources.

Entrepreneurial thinkers see themselves as Business Owners and when company employees act as if they own the company themselves, this is music to C-level executives, customers and shareholders' ears. The trick is to learn how large companies convince employees that their business mission is to enrich the lives of customers rather than just being a producer of products and services (money making machines). I've hired hundreds of employees and the ones that made the most money got it because they were able to see how much value I, as the decision maker, was basing on their work. A word to you contractors out there, base your rate on the value you are providing.

As Business Leaders, one of our highest rewards is when we hear employees act like Business Owners. One way to help employees think like Business Owners is to reward employees heavily on overarching company goals (not conflicting departmental goals). This can be achieved by having common goals benchmarked to specific measurements such as productivity, quality control or even company profits (EBITDA: Earnings Before Interest, Taxes, Depreciation and Amortization), or making sure that there is a certain ROI (Return on Investment) within a certain time period. It depends on what level of stakeholder you want to motivate.

If you're a professional thinking about starting your own business, don't make the common mistake of wasting time and money reinventing the wheel. You have transferable skills and business assets that you may not be able to see on your own. You know the old saying, if you're inside the jar you can't see your own label? The basics of how to set-up and properly manage a business are well known. So reach out to coaches, mentors, mastermind groups and partners to help you clarify your business knowledge and assumptions.

Good entrepreneurs know that when you start (or Transition away from) a business, you must be prepared to lead as well as participate in any and all business activities. You may be called to serve as customer service, operations, IT, HR, or in whatever other capacity may become necessary. As the owner and leader of a company, you want to have the ability to provide whatever the company needs. Employees should know how much you care about them AND the value you can deliver for them. Your employees are also your customers and as with customers, you need to always be thinking how you can help them meet their needs.

When starting a business, particularly a small startup, the owner-manager-employee role you will play requires that you know how to perform in most every position with the exception of those special-skill positions. In fact, most franchisors require that their new franchisees learn every position in the business. When you start out small with limited human resources, the leader must be able to understand each step in the product or service process and be able to fill in if an employee can't work or leaves the company.

Successful leaders know that they must let go of working IN the business and commit to working ON the business. This means leaders need to create their own company leaders that think and act like Business Owners. As I mentioned earlier, that doesn't mean they need to be just like the leader. Studies have shown that diversity in a team brings value by adding a variety of different experiences and insights to the mix. If we want to have the most productive time at work, listen to the person that is most qualified to make a decision, not the person with the most formal authority.

Entrepreneurs are constantly looking at ways to provide more value for their current and new customers, while engaging employees, and thereby improving marketing and sales. They don't care who is right, they just want things to work best for their business. They also know that technology won't replace human-to-human contact. *I've seen so many fortune 100 companies try to solve a people problem by purchasing a new technology. Oftentimes front line employees are confused by having three different systems to go to instead of one because they didn't look at things from the customer's perspective. In this case, customer service is actually reduced instead of enhanced!*

So thinking like a Business Owner, whether you are in a corporate environment or startup, will increase career fulfillment and the bottom line. Signing up for leadership programs helps participants learn things like how to take risks, and how to deal with failure. These programs not only help leaders reach their full potential, these programs help participants have stronger relationships with their customers, employees, and families.

Customer Engagement

Customers are often won or lost based on how they are treated. Customer-facing employees are the best resources to help leadership when the business provides them with the resources they need to do the job. This business has their best interests at heart. If the organization doesn't care about frontline employees, they know it and the customer feels it, too. Resources that interact with customers most frequently are potentially a Business Leader's biggest marketing asset. So how can an organization make the most of these important resources? It's essential that Business Leaders and employees see what they are offering through the eyes of their customers.

Before an organization can move to a customer-centric organization, it needs to identify and understand what communications influence the customer life cycle. Just like everyone is a leader, everyone has a customer. Think about who you serve and how your communications might come across to them. If you're in charge of customer communications or own several businesses, you may benefit creating your own communications and the anticipated customer behavioral states based on the Customer Life Cycle.

Customer Life Cycle

The Customer Life Cycle is based on the behavior change curve which we discuss in a later chapter. The first stage is **Awareness**—how might your customer be aware of what you do? If you're in an organization, you may have a "Town Hall" meeting where each department has an opportunity to express what they do and the value they bring to others. For smaller businesses, you may go to trade shows or perhaps your website comes up for your products or services search results.

In the second phase of the Customer Life Cycle is when your customer is **Considering** purchasing something from you. In this stage, your goal is to help them understand the value of what you offer and what makes you uniquely qualified to help them. This may be done through your sales department, or you may conduct webinars to offer a demo of your services.

The primary purpose of the first and second phase of this life cycle is for your customer to take action and **Purchase** your product or service. Depending on your customer type, this may mean a small purchase like your book, or a larger on-going purchase such as your leadership group.

Once your customer purchases something from you, the next phase is to get them to **Prefer** you over your competitors, or even better than that, find ways for them to be loyal to purchasing products and services only from you. Customer **Loyalty** is the holy grail for all Business Leaders. You see loyalty programs all the time when someone hands you a "buy 10 get 1 free card." There have been many books written on customer loyalty.

The key here is to know what is meaningful to your customer and to give them what they want or need before they ask you. Simple, right? And not always easy. The last phase of the Customer Life Cycle is **Advocacy**. Most businesses measure Advocacy by aiming for a high "Net Promoter Score". A Net Promoter Score is what is calculated every time you answer the question, "Would you recommend this product or service to a friend?" You can't make a customer advocate for you, however you can:

- Go the extra mile for your customers and,
- Ask for referrals from customers at "high points" within the relationship

If any of your customer communications are going to change based on the Customer Life Cycle, make sure everyone on your team is aware of the changes prior to implementing them. This is another important example of what I mean when I say, "working ON your business rather than IN your business." If you have a company of your own or you work as a director in a department, you can map out what your customer sees versus what you do for your customer. Sometimes we get too wrapped up in what we are doing and need to lift our line of sight to see from our customer's perspective. Here is an example of a Customer Line of Sight Model.

Client Line of Sight Model Example

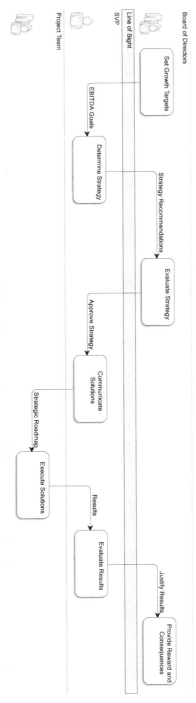

The previous example shows what your activities look like from your customer's perspective (in this case the Board of Directors). This model helps leaders focus on what the customer "sees" during our business activities so that we can be mindful of the customer's experience.

Once you have a good idea of how your actions (or wait time) appears to your customer, you can continue to build your brand. You can use this model to build your brand as a leader, or to build your business brand. This is where we ask questions to uncover the impact our actions have on other, and is especially important for many to advance in their careers, whether it is within a corporation or on their own. Either way, leadership branding essentials include:

1. Know what you believe as a leader and the impact you want to create—this is your leadership stake.

2. Understand your brand as a leader—for what do others say you are the "go-to" person? This is where you can verify if your intended impact is effective.

3. Identify your expertise or competitive advantage as a leader.

4. Learn everything you can about your customers/clients within your market or niche.

5. Communicate the benefits (not features) of your products or services.

6. Challenge the current business model's way of thinking and addressing problems.

When we can see things from different perspectives, we are all the better for it. Although good leaders know how to get things done, great leaders are curious.

Say the C-Word—Curiosity

The world isn't always sure what to do
with us when we're curious.
As if questioning a box they are trying to
check would be bad for them.
Be curious anyway.

-Nina Segura

As a little girl, I remember watching action movies with my mom. I asked, "Why do they wear different-colored hats?" She replied, "The good guys wear the white hats and the bad guys wear the black hats." Again I asked, "Why do the bad guys wear black hats?" My mom said, "To tell the difference between the good guys and bad guys." Still curious, I questioned, "But why are the bad guys bad?" She laughed and then responded with, "I don't know! End of discussion!"

It's 40 years later, and I am still asking that question. What would happen if there weren't black and white hats in the world? What if we were more fascinated with asking questions rather than being afraid of "rocking the boat." What if we spent more time in a three-year-old childlike state of curiosity? This state of being curious is what makes us human **BEings.**

I think most of us are in a constant state of transition. Transitions are rough stuff, and most of us have a definitive way of "how" these transitions should work. We sometimes get stuck when they don't work that way. And, things almost always work in a way different than we initially expect. It's not usually a case of "one size fits all." I'd like you to decide if you are committed to being the leader in your own life AND to achieving success—regardless of how the transition works. **Because no transition works the same way for everyone.** What I am talking about is the idea that curiosity is a way of being. What if we pause the need for a black-and-white answer? What if we just simply ask more questions?

Think about an important question for which you don't have an answer right now. One way we can get an answer is by being more curious. Why don't you, right now, take a deep breath, and close your eyes. It's okay. You can do it. Go ahead and pause for a minute and take a few deep breaths. Now open your eyes and look at an object near you. Take away what you know about it, and instead describe it like you would to a three-year-old alien. What is it? What does it feel like? Who cares about this object? Why is it here? Where else can we put it? How will we use it? When did it get here?

The key to the paradox of being curious and listening to our intuition (our compass) is to be unattached to what you think you already know. This is what makes specific questions from a coach or a mastermind group so powerful. ***When we live the question versus being committed to having a right or a wrong answer, we make room for a transformational experience.***

If you work for an organization and are transitioning to a C-level position, you know that your Crew needs to see you as a Visionary and Thought Leader. So if you have a great strategy in mind, the way to win hearts and minds is the way you ask questions about the gaps within the organization. Helping people based on a need, or gap they have is usually the most effective way of gaining traction. It takes resources to put things into action: financial resources, human resources, equipment and infrastructure, and a plan for moving from the intangible (your plan) to the tangible (the action you will take).

Business Leaders as well as employees need to "see" the value in change so that everyone (including you) can know what is expected of them. Well-thought-out business strategies, including cost benefit analysis and job descriptions, will not only help define job expectations and responsibilities, but should also make clear how each position adds value to those that are impacted by it. Here are some additional thoughts on outlining benefits.

Create a Business Case Full of Benefits

A good business case starts with understanding who is the audience that will be reading it. What do/does the decision maker(s) want(s), and what's in it for them? How are they motivated? What are they afraid of? Lawsuits? Or an increase in errors and omissions insurance for example? These are the considerations we need to keep in mind when we write a business case.

Sometimes those who need to hear our business cases are not only those with authority, it is also important to those who influence those in authority. Identifying who is influential can be determined by watching to whom does the person in authority listen? Or who would care if what you are proposing was done or not? Sometimes we can have all the facts, but we also need to create awareness of the key influencers having impact on our audience.

To summarize, a business case is an information-based tool that supplies a view of the consequences in taking a proposed action, and a good business case will use multiple analytic approaches whether or not an action is taken. Common analytical approaches include: financial components such as a **Cost Benefit Analysis** and **tools from Lean and Six Sigma.** It's also important to remember the human impact associated with the business case, too, because most change initiatives fail when organizational leaders forget to put people first. Perceived value is what truly sells a business case. Now for the fun stuff.

In this area of quantifying benefits, there are two types: hard and soft benefits. A hard benefit, for example, is when you save dollars; soft benefits could be an increase in customer satisfaction. There are two ways to determine **benefits, saves and costs**. In Six Sigma we look at how to improve quality by eliminating unnecessary rework, or by reducing cycle time or reducing customer complaints. Another way is to stop producing more than we need. Here are a few examples:

- Technology (IT) costs: costs of developing a script, or enhancements to existing customer automation.
- Vendor costs: the cost to have somebody else do the work; for example, if a function were outsourced, how much would

a vendor charge us for carrying a specific service?

- Sunk costs: costs that will be incurred regardless of whether or not the project will be pursued; examples include gathering analytical reports; all the costs up to the decision point of go/no-go; all the money and the resources if the project does not get funded.

In summary, when we consider costs it helps if we identify what it costs us now to maintain, change and/or dispose of what we are doing.

Now I'll name a few critical components of a business case. First, **business knowledge**, for example, of what is happening in our industry today, who's impacted by what we are attempting to address, and who are the customers of our output? Also, what new customers can we reach? What new capabilities are available to us? What are the risks and benefits of doing/not doing what we are proposing?

Second, **assumptions** are critical, and most times through the use of a root cause analysis, we can substantiate some of those assumptions.

Third, the **scope** of a project allows us to hone in on a specific problem to determine its solution. In general, we should always attempt to solve problems that are concrete; not like trying to solve world hunger, or create international peace. These are noble goals, but we must define the problem, narrow it down to a specific focus and solve it. This way we increase the chances of success, by attainable goals that can be quantified and measured. If a project is too big then we break it down into smaller projects.

Geography is easy, allowing us to pinpoint specifically the scenario we are addressing, located, e.g., only at the department level, say just the customer service department? Is the scenario just the U.S. or does our business case impact our operational center in Latin America?

And fourth, consider **TIME**, such as that evidenced in rework and opportunity cost: the cost of foregoing alternatives, investments or options if, let's say, we are going to spend one million dollars on a specific project to enhance our technology. We need to compare the return from this investment against other potential returns that we could realize; maybe we could invest that money in rewards and recognition to increase service time performance. The approach of a Cost/Benefit Analysis helps quantify financial benefits and costs for an investment over a specific time period. The benefits are weighed against the corresponding costs. The Cost Benefit Analysis (CBA) will also list "soft" or non-financial costs or benefits. In summary, the CBA will provide an understanding of the net effect of a decision.

Last, consider the **Payback Period**: the length of time required to recover the cost of an investment/action. It is helpful to know exactly what this is before presenting a business case. Most times when management is making capital budgeting decisions, or funding decisions, they want the payback period to be one year or less. Strong business case prioritization processes include a five-year cash flow analysis, an Internal Rate of Return (IRR) and the Net Present Value; that way we can compare the initiatives that are competing for funding at a companywide level. Next, we will discuss how we arrive at some of the cost benefit components. The IRR for an investment is the discount rate for which the total present value of future cash flows equals the cost of the investment.

Regardless of whether you create a formal business case, it's important for you to know how your work benefits your business. For example, many leaders have a good understanding of what their value-to-market is, and also how their offering makes them different from the competition. But they often forget if they get stuck doing administrative tasks or are involved in micromanaging the operations, it can hijack the real value they can provide their company. It's always a good idea to play to your strengths and delegate those tasks that keep you from being the most productive. Bottom line: know YOUR value to the company and the market.

Leaders with best practices will revisit an employee's value during the performance review. However, how many C-level Business Leaders or Business Owners get valuable feedback from a performance review? Even when you are on the top of the pyramid, seek out mastermind groups with people of your caliber so you can be aware of what might need improvement. A person, like a business, could be constantly trying to improve and evolve. If the leader isn't aligned with that belief, then what happens to their company?

Learn How to Process Failure

How do you treat yourself when you make a mistake? I learned (and am continually reminded) to not base my success on something outside my control. This may have been because I was raised in a home where I was constantly told I was stupid. It's taken me years to not reinforce that message internally when I make a mistake. Negative thinking starts at a very early age and on a subconscious level; to evolve both as an individual and a Business Leader, you need to be brutally honest with yourself about your own negative thinking. An important part of being a good coach is helping to facilitate a deeper dive into who you are and what you want and need. When you think about it, who else do you talk to about such personal things?

Here's the deal. If I don't go to yoga or I skip a meal, I am not a very friendly person. So do I really need to send that last email or double-check my text messages? The truth is, when I go against what's best for me, I have different voices in my mind. One says, "Nina, your best changes from time to time." And another from my leadership trainer, **Rick Tamlyn, says, "Nina, Recover! Recover! Recover!!"** Today I continue to work on being more compassionate with myself when I fail. I may not like it; I may have a S@#t storm to clean up, but in the end, I am part of the human race.

Whether you work for a company or have your own business, your business life is not YOU! There is a huge difference between your business failures and who you are. Many businesses fail because the Leadership Team doesn't know how to deal with disappointment! Most of us equate failure with personal shame. It's only later in life that we learn failure is not a personal flaw, but instead is an opportunity to learn and grow. If you are out there playing the game, failure is always a possibility. In fact, one could say that success is most reflected by how you handle your failures, not your success. It's a well-known fact that most self-made millionaires were serial failures before getting it right.

I know disappointment hurts; I've been there, and yet I also know that you are so much more than your temporary disappointments. Learn from failure; become better and move on! Don't let your ego or the expectations of others hold you back or turn you away from pursuing your legacy.

I led many teams to success and with others we fell short. However, I clearly remember feeling lonely and a bit lost in the first few years of business. I felt like somehow I should know how to manage a team. It took me years to realize I needed additional resources, and now I know I am not the only one. I know what it's like to come to work and wonder what the rest of your team is doing. It's hard to be happy at home when things aren't going well at work. However, I know that you can contribute to and be part of a high-performing appropriately self-directed team that is respected and rewarded, AND you don't have to come up with all the answers by yourself.

As a leader you know how important it is to play to your team's strengths in order to create a positive impact. So if you want to know more about your team's SuperPowers, I put together a short SuperPowers assessment just for you (visit: NinaSegura.com-/SuperPowers). By interacting with it, you will better understand your SuperPowers and the SuperPowers of your team, AND you will learn at least one thing that can be done now to cultivate your SuperPowers and get in the "super" flow.

Know thy SuperPowers

> *Everyone is a genius but if you ask a*
> *fish to climb a tree he will live his whole*
> *life thinking he is stupid.*
> *-Albert Einstein*

There are six core Leadership SuperPowers and each of us have various degrees of all of them. It's important that we understand which SuperPower we are most inclined to lead from, so that we can identify a good Crew (SuperTeam) to support us in areas that may be a challenge.

Take a look at the chart of SuperPowers definitions that follow and identify your most resonate SuperPower. You will also notice specific ways to cultivate your SuperPowers by:

1. Increasing your intuition.

2. Learning how to be appropriately vulnerable with your team in order to build trust.

3. Understanding which complementary SuperPowers will help you form your very own SuperTeam!

DIRECTIVE

You have the same **SuperPower** style as Thor, Steve Jobs, and Barbara Corcoran (Directive Leaders).

SuperPowers: You are most effective in times of chaos or crisis, such as in a company turnaround or recovering from a computer failure. You may also be called in to help take control of problems when everything else has failed. You often work best when there is no time for group decision-making. Your SuperPower can often work well in a regulated environment.

How To Cultivate Your SuperPowers: Relationships are more important than results in the long run. Know that everyone comes from a different point of view based on their own personal experience. If you are skeptical about a decision that wasn't made by you, talk to someone you trust about your resistance.

- You may have perfectionist tendencies. Practice taking small risks even when you don't have ALL the details.

- Being appropriately vulnerable may mean that you let yourself make a mistake on a minor detail; the reaction of others may not be as upsetting as you had imagined. Remember the distinction between failing and being a failure.

- Recognize team achievements along the way. To build relationships, team up with a Relational or Flexible SuperPower!

VISONARY

You have the same **SuperPower** style as Professor X, Aung San Suu Kyi, Martin Luther King Jr., and Richard Branson (Visionary Leaders).

SuperPowers: You have the ability to inspire others towards a vibrant vision. You may often see something you thought of years ago now on the market. Typically, you work best in a flexible environment although you may find it hard to complete something without a firm deadline. You can be either introverted or extroverted based on your latest intuitive hit. Your SuperPower is most effective when a new direction or out of the box thinking is needed.

- **How To Cultivate Your SuperPowers**: You are an idea maker so it may be challenging to execute something that wasn't your own idea. Try to find creativity in the work you have now without having to create something from scratch. Inspire others through a team builder all your own! It may be a challenge to eliminate distractions during meetings.

- Your creativity is a great example of using your intuition; help others get in touch with their own!

- Be sure to ask for help focusing on one thing at a time. Also, ask for boundaries to be outlined, as your SuperPower may tend to over-create and forget important deadlines.

- You may prefer for others to figure out the details, so you may want to team up with a Logic or Directive SuperPower!

SYSTEMIC

You have the same **SuperPower** style as Bat Man, Peter Senge, and Marissa Ann Mayer (Systemic Leaders).

SuperPowers: You may love to optimize systems and methods to improve results. You likely take in many details and clearly articulate new paths to success. You may work best in highly ambiguous lines of business. Your first reaction to problem solving may often be organizing the information. Your SuperPower is very useful in the face of mergers or acquisitions. You may be better at creating systems than tactical plans. Your SuperPower typically excels doing strategic work.

- **How To Cultivate Your SuperPowers**: You probably work best when you can create your own system or follow a clear methodology or approach. Your team needs you to support them with effective processes, so make sure others know they can ask for your input in these areas.

- You may not trust your intuition unless it is in an area of expertise or backed by facts. Try reverse-engineering to increase your intuition. Think about how you felt before making a failed decision, then figure out how you can listen to yourself better in the future.

- You may feel vulnerable when operating outside of a system you didn't build yourself. This may create discomfort and defensiveness. When others ask you to operate outside of your own approach, try acknowledging that you are out of your comfort zone. Ask a trusted leader or mentor to share a time when they were out of their comfort zone.

- When there is a need to create a new system, team up with the Visionary Leader to help inspire others to see the value.

RELATIONAL

You have the same **SuperPower** style as Mister Fantastic, Angela Merkel and Oprah Winfrey (Relational Leaders).

SuperPowers: Your SuperPower is connecting with people. You are able to easily create group commitments to meet common goals. You may prefer a consensus-building approach, which can turn into a huge hurdle in times of crisis. When that occurs, team up with a Directive SuperPower! You are usually extroverted and love being in the service with others. This SuperPower works best when their work environment sees the value of tapping into the collective wisdom of the people around them.

- **How To Cultivate Your SuperPowers**: You may not naturally think like an independent business owner and prefer to endlessly socialize an idea or promote another person's idea.

- Team up with a Logical SuperPower to help you understand the importance of details. Your team needs you to remind them about the importance of building key relationships.

- You likely trust your intuition but represent it as one option, instead of the preferred one for yourself. Remember what is important to you. Don't back down when you know you have the best idea.

- You may be the first one to show vulnerability so think about how that might be positively impacting your team.

LOGICAL

You have the same **SuperPower** style as the Black Widow, Mark Zuckerberg and Craig Newmark (Logical Leaders).

SuperPowers: You usually see the tasks that need to be performed in order to meet the goals before anyone else. You often work hard to achieve high performance standards. You are likely task oriented and tend to know how to motivate and reward resources to get work done. Your SuperPower offers leadership that ensures deadlines are met and jobs are completed. You are often great at analysis and not often confused by other people's stories.

How To Cultivate Your SuperPowers: If you're not getting the opportunity to present your logic to the team, find a way to present it in a way that benefits everyone. Team up with a trusted Relational SuperPower to get some helpful hints. While you may be studying the plan for defects or concerns, remember the consequences of over-engineering. Your team needs you to help them manage relevant information to perform together as a team.

- Intuition has a logical place in your life. Doesn't it make sense to use this most natural gift already within you.

- Be vulnerable with someone you trust; it may help you get to your desired outcome. Appropriate vulnerability builds trust in the team and improves outcomes. Look for the opportunity to resolve other's complaints by being very slow with offering your logical solution. Listening to others first may allow them the opportunity to figure it out on their own.

- You may need to team up with a Flexible SuperPower to remember that sometimes "mistakes" can be good things. Team up with a Visionary SuperPower to remember the big picture!

FLEXIBLE

You have the same **SuperPower** style as "Elastigirl, Gamora, Chanel, and the Dalai Lama (Flexible Leaders).

SuperPowers: Your SuperPower provides you with the ability to adapt your leadership style based on the needs of the situation. You can often reach high goals because you have the willingness and know how to take on whatever role is needed. You may have many loyal fans due to your ability to stay positive and encourage the talent of others. Your SuperPower understands how best to adapt style and behaviors to increase results.

- **How To Cultivate Your SuperPowers**: You may reflexively act as the ringleader for all Super Team Members. Your timing and intuition are typically impeccable. Just make sure to check your assumptions. You may not mind what part you play as long as everyone is either getting along or the goal is met. However, it's okay to say the word NO.

- You probably love to learn and help others, so encourage others to know when to share their intuition appropriately.

- You may be filled with humility and may not even be aware of the value that you bring to the team. Increase your ability to be vulnerable by asking for help when you need it and saying no when you need to take care of yourself.

- Team up with a Directive SuperPower when you need the words to ask for additional resources. Team up with a Relational SuperPower when you need words to express that something is no longer working for you.

What are Your Leadership SuperPowers?

So, which of the leadership SuperPowers most resonate with you? Create a discussion with your work family and team about these SuperPowers as an opportunity to share and build trust and support for your personal and professional development. Ask five people who know the impact of your work what they see as your leadership strengths (SuperPowers).

Next present this query to an additional five people (I suggest you pick at least one person who typically doesn't agree with you or sees things differently), and ask them what they think.

- What leadership SuperPowers do you most exhibit?

- Which ones would benefit you to further develop?

- What additional education and training might you require?

- Are there other projects, products, assignments, responsibilities or relationships you can take on or learn more about?

After your initial questions, consider meeting with your internal team or mastermind group:

- Who do you know that might be able to join your Crew and help you become a Super Team?

- When you have made some progress share appropriate (and politically correct) short- and long-term career goals.

- Discuss how you can best implement them in your organization and culture.

- Ask your Crew for feedback on your communication skills.

- Talk about what you can do to develop more effective relationships/partnerships.

So remember Super Leaders do:

1. Access their intuition like gold

2. Are appropriately vulnerable

3. Think like Business Owners AND get their teams to think like Business Owners, too

4. Understand what is happening from their customer's perspective

5. Stay curious

6. Know how to write a business case for change

7. Process their failures

8. Know their SuperPowers.

To find out more about your SuperPowers and the SuperPowers of your team visit: www.NinaSegura.com/SuperPowers

CHAPTER FIVE
COMMON CHALLENGES:
BUSINESS AND LIFE CASE SCENARIOS

It's a bit risky to generalize complex situations, but there are patterns that suggest we humans do share common desires and inhibitions. As a coach, I study these cases and how they can best be handled to reach a solution. Some of the most common stressful and challenging business-life scenarios are:

1. **"The Breakaway Leader."** This is when an individual wants to become free from the decisions of an organizational chain of command and desires to take on the challenge of becoming independent and self-directed. Underlying this natural urge are the risks of uncertainty and failure.

2. **"The Indentured Servant."** One of the most frequent complaints from Business Leaders is having become totally absorbed by the business with no free time and the struggle of distinguishing who they are from what the business does.

3. **"Working Harder, Not Smarter."** Many top executives and owner-operators reach a point where their responsibilities span a multitude of areas and they feel overwhelmed.

4. **"The Fumbled Baton Pass."** Many private companies reach a crisis when the founder or head of the family retires or they become incapacitated. In fact, in this case very few businesses survive a change at the top without an effective Transition Plan.

To give you an idea of how a mentor might go about helping to resolve these common problems, we are presenting a few general case studies. Keep in mind that there is no cookie-cutter approach; it depends extensively on the decision maker's commitment to actually fix the problems as well as the Crew's ability to establish trust and credibility with the client and company staff. In other words, don't try this at home without proper guidance.

"The Breakaway Leader"

- You have always been an achiever and fairly successful at what you take on. You have been working for years as a leader and you think you have a solid grasp on the value your company provides to its customers. You have reached a point where you see ways that can help improve the organization but your ideas are not taken seriously because of the political dynamics. In fact, you begin to see more and more business decisions being made on a political basis and not on what is best for the company, its employees or its customers.

- Your Senior Leaders see you as a potential threat, a bad apple or a heretic and you are no longer one of their fair-haired super stars. You may feel that your future for growth—much less keeping your current position—is in jeopardy. You have several choices: 1) try to move to another department; 2) confront your leaders and try to clear things up; 3) look for employment with another company that would value your skill set; 4) go around your leaders and discuss the problem with someone higher up; 5) start your own business and leverage your skills and knowledge for your own benefit; 6) marry into the owner's family (just kidding).

- Assuming you want to start your own business, your decision will depend on many factors such as:

- Your capabilities as a leader

- Gaps in the market you can fill

- Financial resources

- Your desire and ability to commit to establishing a new business

- Accepting the risk of failure and loss of financial resources

- Your discussions with your significant other about your plans (if you don't have a significant other, find a person whose judgment you trust and confide in them)

Better yet, find a leadership program that can provide a real-world understanding and has specific training for just such situations. For example, a coach would start out by asking some of these deeper-level questions:

- What values are being stepped on at work?

- How might the problem with your leader be showing up in other ways in your life?

- What is another way to look at your situation?

- What values will you be honoring by opening your own business?

- How important is being a Business Owner to your legacy as a leader?

- How might shifting careers impact those around you?

As you can see, these are probing questions as to what the client sees as the immediate problem. But it can go much deeper than that. Maybe other issues are compounding the problem at work or perhaps the client's values, leadership style and goals are not aligned with those of the job or company culture.

This line of open-ended questioning also challenges the client to become more introspective as well as the client's Leader Within to start self-evaluation. The coach invites the client to go deeper, to determine what the client really values and wants out of their personal and professional life; their "dream" goals, interests, and what makes them happy and fulfilled. The coach's job is to help steer the client on the road to self-discovery and if the coach acts also as a mentor, they can provide insights into what leadership, business processes or methodologies might be applied to various situations.

The fact is, we all have a vision of what our life work is supposed to be like, but more often than not, we don't place ourselves in the dream. Well-meaning parents will usually tell their children to find work or a profession they wanted for themselves. Parents aren't always the most objective when it comes to helping their children. There are just too many subtleties that require a convergence of abilities, feelings, and a knowing when something is right for each individual person. When we don't take the time to listen to the Leader Within, it's a trade-off between what our parents or society advises us to do and the calling of our heart, which requires using all of our skills and abilities.

There is a certain cost-benefit when choosing a career. Most often we all make the mistake of taking the position where money, benefits and prestige are the key variables in the cost-benefit; a lot of money means a lot of benefits to choose from. Far too few job applicants do it the other way around: first, consider the benefits and how much personal sacrifice and quality of life it will cost to acquire those benefits. But now, we come to the crucial question: What "benefits" are important to us? And here is where the root of our modern day work-life problems springs from, in my opinion: Some of us in our mid-life today are confused about what really makes us fulfilled. As we get older, what's important to us begins to shift. Those who take the time to dig deep and define what it is you really require from a particular career, and why you require those things, will be all the better for it. Who knows; you might get everything you're wanting.

Truth be told, most of us see the ability to generate income as the pursuit of happiness. There are enough experiences and things that can be purchased to make us happy and entertained...for a while. But true happiness and fulfillment are found on a much deeper level and most often it has nothing to do with consumption, it has much more to do with the alignment of what we do with who we are and what we value.

We are talking about freedom, flexibility, creativity, self-respect, the opportunity to grow and be challenged, the need to feel a part of something greater than ourselves, and on and on. These values lie at the heart of who we are, but it's not always easy to find out who we are; it usually takes quiet, honest introspection and self-evaluation.

In the "Breakaway Leader" scenario, the coach would be looking for how important their client's values of freedom or flexibility are in a business. If they become chafed under the control of a certain leadership style or job description, it might be easier for the client to seek out a position that provides that freedom within the organization. The same goes for other values such as creativity or seeking new challenges. In many seemingly intractable situations, the first tendency might be to run and avoid confrontation, particularly if the power structure is asymmetrical—as it usually is.

So, one of the first and most important steps a coach will take is to guide you through a process of self-evaluation, both within the context of business and personal environments. You may think you want to break away but your real values and needs may not be aligned with the real-life job description that being your own company requires. Going through an assessment will save you a lot of pain and money before setting sail into uncharted waters. It's just good due diligence.

The fact is that you may not be who you think you are. I'll never forget the day in my leadership program that Helen House and the rest of my Leadership Team told me how they experience my impact as a leader. It was very different than what I thought my impact was, and painfully, far different than I wanted.   When people "think" of you, they remember an experience or experiences, and they feel it. This is why knowing who you are as a leader and the impact you are creating around you is so vital.

As a female Business Leader and coach for many male clients, I will go no further than to say helping men learn how to identify and trust their inside world, like their feelings, match their outside world is one of my strengths. I have seen how important this has been for most men when they become confused or unsure of what they really want out of life. After all, they are the brave cowboys, the generals and the swashbuckling river boat gamblers and other antiquated expectations society puts on its young boys.

In fact, one of the major elements of my philosophy is that most men would greatly benefit by being more in touch with their gut feelings or intuition, relieving them from the limited focus on fulfilling the "breadwinner" role. However, that is changing as education, societal expectations and opportunities are trending to more female entrepreneurial leadership roles. Have you sat down and gone through a self-evaluation session that included more than just a multiple question survey?

Those surveys and questionnaires are only tools to build a generalized profile, whereas a coach will challenge who you think you are. They will help guide you to not only define who you are but how best to leverage that knowledge in your business and personal life.

Breakaway Transition Planning—Don't Quit Your Day Job YET

If you are considering striking out on your own as an entrepreneur it can be intimidating, especially when it comes to "financial security." A lifetime job with full retirement and benefits is mostly a thing of the recent past. But capitalism and the United States were not founded on the proposition that citizens have the right to expect financial security. Indeed, our system is based on change, opportunity and the tenacity to take on that challenge.

I've heard aspiring entrepreneurs say, "If she or he can do it, so can I." While the self-confidence is good, you need practical wisdom. Believe me; starting a successful business will test everything you have. Do the due diligence and seek out what you already know. If you have a good idea, are aligned with yourself and your resources and the gaps in the market, you have a good probability of success. When you know deep inside that this is something you must do—you can't afford not to do it! If you believe that failure is a risk, but the worst that can happen is we learn and move on, then you are ready.

Okay, now that the questions of values, alignment and leadership SuperPowers have been analyzed, let's suppose the "Breakaway Leader" decided there is reason to take the leap. Now it's time to take action. The preferred next step is not to leave the job but to plan for the eventual transition once certain conditions are satisfied. This can be difficult if there is an emotional component to the situation, but the next step is critical before the breakaway. I'm talking about business planning.

You may think you have a good idea for your new business but you must do the due diligence of investigating the "feasibility" of your concept. Without going into great detail, you will need to take the following steps to come to an **objective decision** determining if the idea will work for you as well as what the risks are. The following is a general outline of what a business plan typically contains. However, the devil is in the details, particularly when it comes to financial assumptions.

Business Plan Outline

Executive Summary

Company Vision
Company Mission
Industry Analysis Size
The Opportunity
Business Strategy
Target Market and Need
Competition
Marketing and Sales Strategy
Management
Operations
Human Resources
Technology
Products and Services
Development Timeline

Financial Summary
Transformation Strategy
Transition Plan
Summary & Conclusions

Company Overview

Description
Goals and Objectives
Company Competitive Advantage
Legal Description
Research & Development
Trends & Opportunity
Business Interaction Models
Forecasting Models
Revenue Models

Products

Product
Need
Product Strategy
Benefits
Current Stage of Development
Future Plans for Development
Intellectual Property

Services

Service
Need
Service Strategy
Service Profit Chain
Benefits
Current Stage of Development
Future Plans for Development
Intellectual Property

Operations

Strategy

Location(s)
Description of Area(s)
Weather or Disaster Recovery Needs
Business Process Models
Value Stream Maps
Customer Service
Operational Expenses
Staffing and Training
Compensation and Incentives
Administrative and Financial Systems
Administrative Expenses

Technology

Technology Overview
Website Overview
Database Overview
Technology Process Models
System Interaction Models
Operating Platforms
Other Software Applications
Hardware

Economics of the Business

Assumptions
Sales Projections and Growth
Demand and Price Elasticity
Cost of Services
Gross and Operating Margins
Fixed and Variable Costs
Expense Breakdown
Months to Breakeven
Months to Positive Cash Flow
Burn Rate
Sensitivity Analyses Summary

Development Milestones

Development Strategy

Milestones and Action Plan
Development Timeline
Development Expenses

Industry & Market Analyses

Industry Overview
Industry Trends and Growth Patterns
Industry Participants
Company Niche
Market Analysis
Marketing Concept
Market Characteristics
Market Size and Trends
Target Market Trends and Growth Patterns
Business Market Demographics
Customer Profiles
Size of Firms-Private Industry

Competitive Analysis

Overview
Direct Competitors
Indirect Competitors
Product Line Competition
Service Line Competition
Market Share Analysis
Comparative Analysis
Competitive Advantages

Marketing and Sales Strategy

Marketing Strategy Overview
Positioning
Advertising
Public Relations, Publicity, and Promotions
Media Objectives and Strategy
Marketing Budget
Growth Strategy
Strategic Alliances

Joint Marketing

Agreements
Sales Strategy
Sales Process Description
Pricing Models

Management

Organizational Structure
Management Team
In-House Management-Job Descriptions
Management compensation
Board of Advisors
Board of Directors
Professional Advisors:

        Legal
        Accounting
        Technology
        Marketing
        Public Relations
        Insurance
        Human Resources
        Other

Critical Risks

Competitive Risks
Technological Risks
Management Issues
Macroeconomic Environment
Staffing Concerns
Industry Health
Seasonality and Cyclical Trends
Legal Factors
Funding Concerns

Offering (Optional)

Capitalization
Investment Requirements

Valuation of Business
Offer
Stock Allocation
Return on Investment
Use of Funds

Financial Projections

Financial Summary
Sources and Uses of Funds
Projected Rates & Income Forecast Initial Opening Year
Estimated Potential Market Penetration
Penetration Rates
Financial Assumptions
Income Statements
Cash Flow Statements
Balance Sheet
Breakeven Analysis
Sensitivity Analysis
Financial Ratio Comparison

Appendices

Management Resumes
Detailed Financials
Product Images
Customer Line of Visibility Diagrams
Workflow Diagrams
Office and Manufacturing Layout
Website Image Captures
Licenses
Letters of Intent
Other Pertinent Data

Please note, most private companies do not publish their financials. Without a doubt, private company financial reports are highly susceptible to errors and omissions, planned and otherwise. As a result, you need to do some detective work to develop real-world financial assumptions. Usually, this is a job for a professional who understands financial modeling. Moreover, you need to define the business model (how the company generates income) and the financial model (what that income is and how it's categorized along with KPIs— Key Performance Indicators). Once the business plan is complete, then and only then should any decision be made to "cut the cord."

Here is a fact you can take to the bank: if you have a good idea and a credible business plan, there will always be funding available, either from institutions or private equity investors.

Another critical aspect of having a credible business plan is determining what to do when you have a reluctant significant other. Although they will see your passion and hope for the future, they may be very hesitant to move forward with your dream. However, if they see the plan, the chance they will get onboard is greatly enhanced, although even the best plans and ideas may not be enough. That is where working with a business coach can help you create some financial forecasting and a strong backup plan so that you can make the best choice.

I don't care what anybody says, there is always an element of luck out there and that is usually a function of commitment and time. Therefore, you must have a strong **ACTT Blueprint** as mentioned previously to fall back on.

Top 20 Reasons Startups Fail

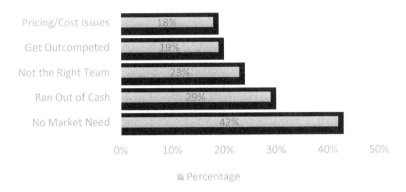

Take a look of the top three reasons for business failures. A well-done business plan will help avoid those killer problems. However, the third one, "Not the right team," can be problematic. This is where developing a "Crew" should come before developing a "Team."

As discussed in earlier chapters, a "Crew" is not a "Team." It may or may not be made up of employees. (This is where you may benefit by coming to a leadership retreat like the ones we do at www.BusinessCoachingOnDemand.com. (Shameless plug I know!)

Remember, typically, a Crew is comprised of experienced, like-minded Business Leaders and professionals who can help provide unbiased experienced and honest input. Further, "cross pollination of ideas" from other Business Owners. Members of a good Crew have "been there and done that." They understand the subtleties and challenges of operating a business. Besides, there are areas that owners need to be careful with when discussing their plans with employees. Indeed, it can be "lonely at the top," which is why having mastermind groups and a good Crew is so important. As always, re-inventing the wheel is not an efficient use of time. Besides, the mistakes you can avoid can save you a ton of money, time and emotional capital.

The formation of a Crew should come before the business because there is a tendency to select friends or people who talk the talk but don't walk the walk. Having experienced and honest input from others can only help with the selection of key staff; this is particularly true if you are new to the business and depend heavily on those with prior experience, as you may not be the best judge if your employees are doing their jobs properly. Even the largest and most complex companies aim to have a strong Crew within their Board of Directors.

In summary, before "breaking away," it's important to take an honest analysis of your true values and what gives you fulfillment before you act on the need to leave the "security" of being an employee and take on the risks of being an entrepreneur. Next, you need to do the due diligence on your idea and be as objective as you can in assessing the viability of your idea and its ability to meet your needs. Finally, before making the jump, make sure you have developed a good Crew to leverage their experience and input. You don't have to agree with everything they suggest, but it helps to keep your mind open. When you are the boss, you tend to feel you have to be right all the time.

"The Indentured Servant"

Many aspiring Business Leaders don't fully understand the level of commitment it takes to get a business up and running. It's your baby and when it cries, you jump! In fact, when a startup blossoms into a success, growth can bury an owner. They need to see to the daily operation, hire new people, develop a training program, watch the Key Performance Indicators (KPIs), and make sure the customers are always happy. When the doors shut at the end of the business day, the Leadership Team may find they are constantly dealing with business issues in their head. In fact, growth can be a real challenge, particularly if the owner is a micro-manager and doesn't trust his staff to do the job right and keep the customers happy. He may see them as just putting in their time to get their paycheck, and only thinking about what they will do on the weekend.

When employees see the boss trying to do everything and not being comfortable letting them assume responsibility, they will naturally pull back and make matters even worse as there aren't enough hours in the day to see to all the tasks required to run a business. This tendency to micro-manage is the principal reason that small businesses stay small.

Leaders must understand that they are the conductor of an orchestra. Their job is to hire the right people, have a strong training program and motivate people to take an ownership attitude about the business. The owner, just like a conductor, helps to direct the total operation, not run it. As the old saying states: "A good leader trains him/herself out of their job." In other words, a good leader learns how to inspire, motivate and train. It's not rocket science, but it does take some training. Unfortunately, most Business Owners may not have had leadership training. In fact, some new owners will copy the leadership styles they have been exposed to as an employee thinking that is the way it should be done.

When owners complain about losing their lives to their business, they are likely not working ON their business as much as IN their business. **They need to develop stronger multi-dimensional leadership competency and know when to delegate responsibilities and accountabilities to their organizational structure.** They might not understand that there are ways to monitor performance without being directly involved. The most critical transition for a small business is to become a formalized and delegated organization with the management tools of formalized policies and procedures, job descriptions, Key Performance Indicators (KPIs) and a management information system that allows leaders to direct, hold people accountable and make sure the business stays on track. Once the business tools and systems are in place, a business can start to grow while offering the Business Leader some relief and more freedom for the other aspects of their life.

"Working Harder, Not Smarter"

This statement always sounds so obvious. Who wouldn't want to work smarter? Yet many Business Leaders get stuck in the trap of working harder instead of thinking of better ways to work. Well, human nature likes the familiar; work habits can become ingrained and the inertia to overcome that complacency can be challenging.

Over the past few decades, technology has come out with some amazing productivity enhancements. In fact, the workplace continues to evolve. However, the rapid advances in technology make it difficult to keep up. In fact, its rapid advance may be keeping some executives from buying new solutions, as they can become antiquated within months. However, one of the main jobs of leadership is to always be searching for ways to improve the customer and employee experience to increase sales and profits. But it's not always just technology that allows working smarter.

Perhaps as important as improving our company's technology is looking for ways to innovate and adapt to increasing competition while tapping into social media and big data. Even so, innovation and adaptation require a collaborative environment to leverage the knowledge and insight across the enterprise. This collaborative and transparent environment may require some new leadership techniques that foster open discussion and creativity. Business Leaders need to develop stronger leadership skills in how to facilitate brain-storming sessions, building their own Crew, thereby improving productivity and ultimately increasing profits.

Further, technology must first be aligned with business goals and objectives. This requires the participation of stakeholders across the company as well as the customer stakeholders. Social and mobile media are powerful new forces that are demanding new ways of gathering data and driving sales. However, developing these new strategies is often beyond the knowledge and experience of top level executives, who can even become obstacles to moving forward. Once again, this is why having an outside perspective while making improvements is so important because if the process of making change is botched, it can make our work environment even more difficult to get people onboard on the next attempt.

In summary, working smarter requires a blending of new leadership skills that focus on knowing what leadership role to step into, clearly defining the objectives of new initiatives to achieve innovation, and the leveraging of new technologies that are aligned with the company vision and mission. For many leaders, these new leadership skills require training and may even be counter to the way they have functioned in the past.

"The Fumbled Baton Pass"

A vast majority of small to mid-size businesses are family owned and operated. But what happens when the founder and directing force of the founder is ready to retire or becomes ill? Often, the founder sees the business as their life's accomplishment and an extension of who they are. In addition, it's rare that instructing family members makes for a good teacher-student relationship. In fact, many sons or daughters of business founders don't want to live the life they have seen their parent(s) live and how it can totally absorb one's life.

Of course, there are many other factors that may make it difficult or impossible to get family members to follow in the footsteps of their relative/founder. As I eluded to previously, this is mainly due to not having a solid Transition Plan in place.

It's sad to see a successful family company that has made the world a better place and provided a good living for its owners wither away for lack of a good plan. However, times are changing and the idea of owning a business—particularly an established one—is very appealing to the next generation. In fact, the family business is a wonderful platform from which to grow and take a business to the "next level."

But it doesn't just have to be a family member to whom you hand-off the business. Key employees who have shown they are capable and willing to take command can also be chosen to take over. In fact, one of the best ways for a Business Owner to pass the torch is to either sell the business to key employees or keep the business and delegate the operation while receiving a passive income and benefits derived from the continued operation of the business. Either way, **it takes advanced planning and training to have a smooth transition.** This is particularly true if the business is heavily dependent on the founder's personality, skills and contacts.

Of course, most of us rarely prepare for the unexpected. If you are a Business Owner, have you asked yourself what would happen to the business if you became incapacitated and were still alive? Would there be no life insurance, and you and your family would be even more dependent on the business? Part of the responsibility of Business Leaders is to identify and plan for risks.

Think about it this way, it's not just about your family; it's also about the families of your employees who might be at risk, and those of your customers and your shareholders (if you have them). If you are a micro-manager and are the driver of your company, you and your employees are at risk if you have no plan in place. By the way, when I say "plan," I mean a written Transition Plan that doesn't leave room for much interpretation on who is responsible for what.

In my experience, having such a plan in place makes a profitable company have more value when it comes time to sell. Most investors don't want to be active participants in running a company, particularly if they are not familiar with the industry. However, if they know that they can be "passive" investors and expect a return on their investment, it's much easier to raise capital or sell the business.

In summary, whether planning for retirement or just prudent risk management, developing a comprehensive Transition Plan is some-thing far too many businesses don't have.

All of the previously mentioned case studies represent some of the typical areas where most companies need help. However, the "bottom-line" is that there are ways to immediately capture and implement a good plan without having to disrupt the daily workings of the company.

Recent times of company streamlining and evolution to meet the demands of globalization, competition, new technologies and changing consumer habits has let loose a cadre of former employees who are expert independent business consultants and coaches that can add real value to a company in a project-by-project context. In fact, running lean can put a strain on staffing, as it's not cost effective to try to devise solutions and implement them when the way to solve the problems are already known. Yes, it will cost money to acquire knowledge and expertise, but how much time and money will it cost without the proper knowledge and expertise? Besides, coaches are independent contractors and provide lower costs and flexibility than in-house advisors, since when the Transition Plan has been completed, they move on.

In most companies, the inner dynamics and the myopia of being too close, make it often a wise thing to seek a qualified, objective outside perspective. Customers, employees and professional coaches can only make a difference if there is an atmosphere of open-mindedness, confidential transparency and the commitment to improvement.

CHAPTER SIX
HOW DOES A COACH BENEFIT THE CLIENT?

Thinking is the place where intelligent actions begin. We pause long enough to look more carefully at a situation, to see more of its character, to think about why it's happening, to notice how it's affecting us and others.
-Margaret J. Wheatley

Business Leaders may search far and wide for ways to transform their company; however, what they might need is an objective and qualified coach. After all, there are only so many options for change that a team can implement without reaching within for the answers. Coaching typically pays off when clients:

- Need to pause and refocus on their purpose.
- Are in the midst of change and need time to make conscious choices.
- Are ready to go to that next level of leadership.
- Need to influence their peers, board of directors or collaborate with colleagues.
- Want a Plan B.

Most Business Leaders and entrepreneurs are limited to where they can seek objective council and input free from internal political factors. The people they work with may tell them what they want to hear, while their families may be supportive but may not be objective. The wise leader learns that they must have someone or some advisory group to act as a sounding board as well as a source of information and insight.

Identifying Personal and Business Goals

In the USA, we love to talk about "the land of the free," but is this the reality of most workers? How prevalent is indentured servitude and work-life inflexibility? Or perhaps does it just feel like it sometimes? I think, the higher the pay, the more the indentured (schedule inflexibility) we can become. Our school system teaches us how to adapt to boredom and regimen. Few of us are made passionate or clear about our lives as we pass through all levels of institutional education. To this day, education is all about preparation to survive in a post-World War II industrial age. What would the world be like if we were taught how to *be?* Be ourselves, be in relationship with one another? Have stronger collaboration and negotiation skills? What would the world be like if we knew our personal values and learned to listen for the values of others?

Personal and professional goals and values are established over a long period of time, initially by parents, schools, peers, and more increasingly, the media. We no longer live in a time of obvious job classifications such as lawyer, doctor, nurse, teacher, chemist, etc. No, the choices and opportunities have far outpaced everyone's ability to know what they are, or might become in the near future.

We do things backwards: fit our aspirations to "what they should be," not what they might have a passion or special aptitude for. So, it usually isn't until later in life that we may truly know what our "calling" is and how to reconcile our inner values and feelings with what we spend 90% of our lives focused on—the job we're done with, and then we begin hating ourselves.

Okay, to be fair, the past system worked fairly well, as long as the values of the culture were able to align citizens with the desired work-life outcome. Having a steady job, getting married, raising a family and being able to purchase more doodads worked for a span in history. But things are changing. A coach can help focus the client on what they really want and help them build and execute a plan to get there.

While we may spout the old party line of "hard work and dedication," the reality of what motivates us may be very different from what drove the last generation. And that does not mean it's a negative. Indeed, some might say that developing self-potential and self-awareness is moving up the chart of desirable, intangible goals. Who can say that's a bad thing?

We could say that as technology, globalization, and raising billions of people out of subsistence living has helped produce a growing awareness and desire to live life as we please, as long as it doesn't hurt anyone else. Indeed, we are moving up Maslow's Pyramid.

Self-Actualization
(Purpose, Potential)

Esteem Needs
(Confidence, Respect)

Social Needs
(Love, Acceptance, Groups)

Safety Needs
(Health, Employment, Stability)

Physiological Needs
(Food, Water, Sleep)

Maslow's Pyramid or Hierarchy of Human Needs was developed in 1943 by psychology professor Abraham Maslow. It demonstrates that as humans, most of us attempt to move up the pyramid after achieving each level of need. Of course, each individual defines when they need to move up to the next level or stay where they are. Business coaches work in the top levels of this pyramid as we guide clients through a series of discovery assessments to identify values, purpose and goals and test those client beliefs.

Making it Real

- How well is your business strategy working?

- How well are your business and personal goals going?

- Which business practices of yours conflict with your values (if any)?

Once a client is Aligned with their personal and professional goals, they can focus on executing their short-, intermediate and long-term goals that align with their legacy as a leader and revisit their progress with their coach.

Evaluating the Current State of the Business

A business coach may put on their mentorship hat from time to time and discuss business with the client. They will delve into the business, marketing, financial models, processes and policies, the market and competition and review the business plan. During the analysis of the business, the mentor will probe for strengths, problems and areas of concern. Most often, there are problems AND solutions that the client is not aware of yet. However, a good mentor will not talk about solutions until all the facts are in. Depending on the industry, most common business-related problems are (not in order of impact):

- Lack of leadership development

- Growing capacity

- Poor team work (lack of Crew)

- Low profitability

- Unclear expectations

- Retention Strategies - too much turnover

- Strategies and tactics for changing markets

It's not uncommon to find that the client's business problems are not related to the business itself. Sometimes there are other personal issues that get in the way of the client being able to function well in the business. Once the coach has demonstrated their professionalism and nonjudgmental approach while interacting with the client, the client usually opens up about tangential issues that they can't or won't talk about with others. It's like confiding in the stranger at the bar beside you. Who do you turn to with personal issues? Remember, big boys and girls don't cry and are always winners, right? NOT!!!

Responsible leaders only multiply their pain when things are going wrong. *The lines between our personal and business life are blurred; unhappiness in either can affect both.*

At this point, it's still too early for the mentor or coach to make any suggestions; however, now that the coach has a general idea of what the client's values, goals and perceived problems are, it's time to introduce the client to a Crew of peers, other Business Leaders, to provide additional input and more Q&A. This is one reason that mastermind groups work.

Introduction to the Group of Business Peers—the "Crew"

As discussed previously, our business coaches set up a series of assessments in the discovery phase including one-on-one time with the client. After that, our client is matched carefully with others in their mastermind group. Our mastermind group, along with the coach, acts as our client's Crew by asking powerful questions, brainstorming and oftentimes helping them with introductions and resources not already at their disposal. During this process, the client will see AND FEEL the value of not being isolated and having direct access and counsel from other leaders who will "tell it as they see it." They may be right or wrong, but a free-flowing discussion has a cathartic effect and exposes the client to the experience and knowledge of other leaders. Indeed, it's far too easy to become isolated with company communications filtered through agendas and not receive the straight talk that can be the catalyst for your leadership to become better.

Develop a Personal-Business Alignment Plan

Now it's time to analyze the alignment of personal and company goals and address areas of conflict or potential conflict. This can take form in a change of organizational structure, policies and procedures, and change of personnel. In fact, it might even lead to the client deciding to pursue another path. The primary goal of a business coach is to help the client live on purpose. When we are fulfilled, we are positive and when we are positive we make our world a better place.

Design the ACTT Blueprint and Help with the Implementation

The coach and the client along with suggestions from the peer group (a.k.a. the Crew) will together develop the **ACTT Blueprint** and help implement identified changes. The best ideas can fail and even backfire if not implemented properly. In fact, a recent study has shown that most new company initiatives fail because of poor implementation and follow-through on the part of top leadership. Let's admit it, change is hard even when we want it.

Ongoing Mentoring and Support

The coach now evolves into a mentor to the client as the **ACTT Blueprint** is implemented, or to act as a sounding board for any top-level issues the client would like to discuss. Also, the peer group (Crew) will come into play when needed. However, anytime a problem comes up that the client wants to discuss, it's important that the coach has an intimate understanding of the client and the business so they can provide valuable input and advice—no matter what the client needs.

Bottom-Line

Your coach and the Crew are there to help you become a purposeful leader in your personal and professional life. This usually results in a strong impactful and more profitable business that provides more value to your customers and employees, which results in a corporate culture of happiness and harmony. Does that sound too good to be true? Why shouldn't it be true? You deserve a good life you know.

CHAPTER SEVEN
MEASURING THE VALUE OF A COACH

The main goal of a coach is to provide a transformational space for their client to be who they've always wanted to be, to achieve their goals, whether that be more profit, more free time to pursue other interests, or whatever helps to create happiness and fulfillment. So how do you know when you are happy? Is it measured by how well you sleep? Is it evidenced by your general attitude toward life? Whatever it is, it boils down to...the F-word, your *feelings*.

Transformation is hard to measure (maybe there is an increase in serotonin or some other physiological way to measure it), but I can't see you standing in front of the mirror in the morning and pulling out a "fulfillment-meter" to measure your blood to find out if you're happy or not. There are other ways to measure your fulfillment by gauging if new improvements to the business action plan have been successful. The following are some considerations toward that goal:

1. The cost of re-inventing the wheel. Anytime you can bypass the hard lessons that have been solved by others, the better.

2. How much time might it take you to figure out how to properly organize your company for optimum profitability?

3. Lost productivity and the cost of rework.

4. How much money is lost due to a poor training program that can be measured in lack of productivity?

What is rework? It is one of the most insidious costs to poor leadership and is usually not tracked. The first time the widget was built or the service was not performed properly, the company still paid for the labor, materials, general and administrative costs and all other related operational cost. Now, if the goods or services have to be made or performed again, the company has to pay for it a second time! But to add insult to injury, while the rework is being done, the company also loses customer and employee satisfaction and labor costs that could have been producing something valuable the first time! In other words, rework due to lack of proper training or lack of quality control can cost the company three times what it costs to produce their output correctly the first time! It shows up as lost productivity but it instead is a reflection on poor leadership.

Hiring the Right People

What about the cost of hiring the wrong people? It can take months or even years to find (or develop) the right people for the particular job. Not having optimized and consistent talent development and work-flow processes in place along with competent people can greatly affect productivity, employee and customer satisfaction and raise costs resulting in lower profits.

Turnover Costs

The average employee can cost so much money to replace in the form of advertising, screening, training and HR staff costs, not to mention having to turn away business if short on staffing.

Recent employee satisfaction surveys suggest that the vast majority of employees are not happy with their employers. In fact, many highly skilled workers prefer to become independent contractors just to avoid having to become absorbed into a corporate culture they can't identify with. Also, many capable employees will choose not to move up in the company to avoid politics and excessive work expectations for managers (notice I said managers—not leaders).

Opportunity Costs

If leadership is not up on its game when it comes to developing its human capital and its ability to participate fully in new and existing technologies coming on-stream, they may miss opportunities as well as lose market share. There is a "War for Talent" out there and having a strong Crew can help attract and keep those key employees.

Profitability, Reputation and Company Value (For Sale or Mergers and Acquisitions—M&A)

If leadership is not optimizing its profitability, it can reduce its value for any resale, its ability to access needed capital, attract investors, and compete with the growing global products and services.

The Intangible Benefits Measured by Self-Assessment

As an owner or leader, how do you *feel* when your company is doing well, when employees and customers are happy, and when you see employees develop and grow? How does it *feel* to see your wealth grow while feeling you are a valued member of society? How does it *feel* to see your family happy and moving along life's road of discovery? As the once familiar TV ad stated: *"Priceless."*

When you are on the receiving end of those positive chemical messages in your brain, the feeling is more real than what can be measured on your profit and loss statement. The next time you purchase a new toy or enjoy a new experience, take note of how you feel and why you feel that way. When you fully understand that your fulfillment is based on honoring your purpose as a leader and living your values, Doctor Maslow will be shaking your hand as you arrive at the top level of his pyramid.

CHAPTER EIGHT
CONSIDER:
HOW IMPORTANT IS YOUR LEGACY AS A LEADER?

On a scale from one to ten (ten being the most) how much of your life is about living your legacy? Is it really your goal to retire in comfort without positively impacting the next generation? I trust that your Leader Within knows that your purpose is much greater that leaving behind a bunch of garage sale items (no offense).

Don't get me wrong, I'm not making a judgment about what your life should be based on. I only ask that you honestly consider what really makes you *feel* fully alive. In my experience, happy is good, but feeling fulfilled is what life is all about. The feeling of fulfillment comes from deep inside your soul and might just scare you a little bit.

When you live and work in our modern American culture, it's too easy to confuse happiness with fulfillment; but they feel different. One is transitory and the other deeply penetrates your persona and provides a more meaningful context for your life's purpose. When we know our purpose, we may have fear and anxiety about it. The trick is to "step on our fear and do it anyway.

> *F-E-A-R has two meanings: 'Forget Everything And Run' or 'Face Everything and Rise.' The choice is yours.*
> *-Zig Ziglar*

So I challenge you to pause long enough to hear your Leader Within. Listen to how certain activities or actions make you feel. For example, I had a client say that his employee told him that they were able to pay off their car based on a bonus they received. My client said it was the best bonus he ever gave an employee. In other words, fulfillment is beyond a temporary "fix."

Being a leader in business offers you the opportunity to obtain most of the earthly benefits if you are good at your business. But too many get stuck on the superficial level as the only goal. When you can Align and connect your goals with the hierarchy of fulfillment your own and others, you will be so much richer and truly feel successful.

How do You Think You and Your Business Will Change Over the Years?

Of course, not only your business but interpersonal and social conditions will also change. Some developments you probably are aware of and some may be a surprise for you. It's natural. Just know what motivates you today may not have the same affect in the future. In the same way, what drives your customers will also change.

A business is a means of not only providing for your survival, it is also a way for you to really live. For you to have the opportunity to be beyond a pyramid of human needs. The best practice for Business Leaders is to create an organizational mechanism that is scalable and sustainable by analyzing what is happening now and what potential changes might and should happen in the future. We call that "enlightened self-interest" or based on what I learned from Peter Senge "Double-Loop- Learning."

Most successful Business Leaders feel the responsibility they have to their employees and customers alike. However, leaders need to be able to dedicate their time and effort to pause and refresh themselves so that they can see their business with new eyes and stay alert for present and future needs.

Good leaders understand that all levels of employees can offer a valuable resource from which they can draw upon. In fact, larger organizations are creating "entrepreneur groups," to tap into the insights and ideas of employees who have different perspectives than does the insolated "C-Suite." One of the best ways to do that is to designate a group of employees across the organization to participate in periodic brainstorming sessions (where there are no wrong ideas) about how the company can improve, innovate and adapt.

I am not afraid for God is with me. I
was born for this!
-Joan of Arc

Identify Your Fears and Insecurities, and their Root Causes

The unknown can be as exciting as it can be menacing. Most human beings don't like uncertainty, particularly in a society that talks about pensions, annuities, and long-term investing and planning. Just imagine how our almost 1000 generations of Homo sapiens lived: meal-to-meal and then planting season to harvest time. Insecurity is deeply rooted in our DNA and that is one reason most of us always keep an eye on the future.

In recent years, job insecurity has become a fact of life at all levels of employment. Almost all of us have either had the experience of being laid-off, downsized or fired. We hear horror stories of hard-working and talented people "losing everything." So, what is "every-thing"? Did they die, disappear or just fade away? What are we really afraid of, living on our family's couch? If your family of origin is like mine, I completely understand that concern, but that's what friends are for.

If you check with most people, they have been terminated from their employer at some point, and they are still living and adapting. So what is the fear we have about losing our current position? Is it that we will lose our self-image or self-respect? Is it that we will lose our special status? Is it because we might lose the home, the car and our ability to consume? Bottom line: It's all about being ready to be pushed out of our comfort zone and fearing the criticism that comes _if_ we do or don't meet the challenge.

What do you fear about the future?

What do you have control over?

What can you do to reduce the anxiety of your fears?

Your Future

Focusing too much on the future and establishing future expectations, although an important survival instinct, can make living in the moment (the only reality) less enjoyable. The best you can do is to let yourself envision your ideal future and identify what strategies you could implement to meet them. Trust in your abilities to adapt and realize that nobody and nothing can take your true values away. This is one of the things I admire about my friend, Shani. She doesn't trust the wind; she trusts her "wings."

What is Holding You Back from Achieving What You Really Want?

First of all, do you have goals that you are striving to achieve? If not, do you know what you will not tolerate? An important business practice is to develop, track and update your own Transition Plan. Sadly, most leaders don't have a formalized plan. They will usually tell you: "I have it in my head." Well, do others in your business have the same vision as you? How can you direct, inspire and motivate your employees if they don't share a common vision of what the company mission is (not what it should be)? Is it just to "keep the doors open" and the paycheck coming in or is there more to it than that?

Yes, people work for a paycheck, but they want to live, too, and not merely survive. Everyone will be more productive when their leader knows and respects what motivates them other than money.

What do Most People Want from their Work-life?

Recent studies done by Gartner Inc. and Inc. Magazine revealed some surprising results of a survey of over 100,000 employees from a wide variety of organizations and industries by listing compensation toward the bottom of the employee engagement list. Of course, their priorities may not represent how you feel. But what the survey does show is that many employees already understand that their work-life requires much more than just a wage and benefits.

A Business Leader who understands the heart of the matter will get to know what motivates key leaders within their organization. Understanding the need to drill deeper than just job performance will allow the company culture to grow and prosper. Based on my research and the research of others, below you will find what we believe are the top ways to improve employee engagement:

1. Employees want transparency.

2. Employees want to be a part of a greater purpose.

3. Employees want the resources necessary to do what is expected of them.

4. Employees want to feel that at least one person they work with consistently cares about them.

5. Employees want the ability to influence.

6. Employees want to be appreciated.

7. Employees want to be developed, not criticized.

8. Employees want flexibility.

9. Employees want to feel successful.

10. Employees want to be rewarded for a job well done.

I can just see old-school managers rolling their eyes. However, today, it appears that we continue to move up the pyramid of needs. Can we do it? Of course we can, and we will!

Obstacles Smobstacles

- As a Business Leader, what obstacles are holding you back from who you want to be personally and professionally?

- What are you really afraid of?

- Who might support you overcoming your fear?

- How do you want your employees to engage with you and your business?

The internet is a gold mine of information not only in research but also for finding experts who can help solve your problems without your having to invent your own solution. A good way to consider whether to do the research yourself or hire an outside coach or consultant to determine how much your time costs the company. Figure out how many hours it would take you to solve the problem properly as well as what other activities you could be doing for the company rather than spending time on research.

One of the great benefits of the unstable employment environment is the vast number of experienced, trained and educated subject-matter experts out there. In fact, the "gig economy" is growing by leaps and bounds. Many highly trained and experienced professionals are finding new freedom by selling their knowledge and experience as an independent consultant. Moreover, the internet allows us the ability to match-up client requirements and providers of expertise without the need to be on site.

Breakaway Due Diligence

Don't be deceived, if you are looking to get away from having a boss, being a Business Owner won't do it for you. As a Business Owner, your customers and employees become your new "bosses." It's more about what you are heading towards (versus running from). Yes, owning your own company can provide flexibility but it takes a lot of work and knowledge to get to that point. Most entrepreneurs have special skills and something that differentiates their abilities from the competition. But what many do not have are the tools to properly organize, price and lead a business on a daily basis.

Operating a business is not just about being able to produce a service or product. It's much more about knowing why you want to do it and the impact you want to have on others. There is a lot to learn and most of those lessons can be expensive if learned the hard way. Here is a common and costly example.

Most Business Owners think that a bookkeeper or accountant is there to make sure expenses and taxes are paid on time. And, oh yes, if a profit is generated. However, bookkeepers and accountants won't help you with financial modeling and pricing strategies like a business coach or consultant would. For example, company pricing should be first based on "market pricing" and then the company cost structure. This *engineering of profit* is basic but most small and even medium-sized businesses don't understand this crucial fact.

Often, a startup company thinks they are doing great. People want the product or service, and often there is not enough money to pay all the bills—particularly labor costs and labor taxes. If these Business Owners aren't able to properly keep costs in check and produce the profit margin necessary to allow growth, your bookkeeper or accountant won't help you. Far too often, a rookie Business Owner thinks the accountant will provide good financial projections and support but that is usually not the case. Accountants are taught tax-based accounting and not managerial accounting, which is based on how to run a company "by the numbers."

If you are thinking of making the break, don't view it as just about having a good idea or employing smart people. It's much more than that and you would be well advised to hook up with a professional business coach or consultant specialized in startup scenarios before making a commitment that will consume you and your money if you don't have your ducks in a row. Sure, a professional consultant will cost you money, but one way or the other, reinventing best practices is much riskier and costlier when you go at it alone.

Question for the Breakaway Candidate

What is the worst that can happen to you if you set sail on a new course? I want you to be realistic and reduce the risk of making a rash decision that you might regret. Once you have determined your goals and how those line up with your personal values and aspirations, the next step is to develop a comprehensive plan that includes credible financial assumptions and the all-important SWOT analysis.

A SWOT analysis is an acronym for Strengths, Weaknesses, Opportunities and Threats.

Once the plan is put together, it's time to shoot holes through it. You don't want the imagined promise of your desires realized to cloud your vision, and that is yet another reason to hook up with a professional coach to provide input on your SWOT.

In my experience, it's not uncommon that after the business plan and SWOT analysis has been completed, the urge to breakaway is tempered by reality. And that is much better than putting your heart, soul and resources into a dream that may not have a solid probability of becoming successful. We are emotional beings and we need to temper our emotions with sound judgment. That said, how many times have we heard the siren's song: "They said it couldn't be done...but we did it anyway!"

No doubt, you should trust your intuition, but success will depend largely on your circumstances and your risk tolerance. If you are single with no children, being on the losing side of the bet becomes just a "learning experience." However, if you have others along for the ride, make sure the gang considers what the worst outcome could be and confront it, taste it, smell it and then come up with a plan. You can't believe how that helps send the fear packing.

Leadership SWOT

A Leadership SWOT (Strengths, Weaknesses Opportunities & Threats) supports your development as a leader, whether or not you are a Business Owner or work within an existing organization.

SWOT Analysis for _____

Date: _____

	Positive	Negative
Internal	**Strengths** What do others say you do well? What do you know you do well? What is unique about you? What are you most proud of personally/ professionally?	**Weaknesses** What could you do better? What do you need to avoid? What do others say you can improve?
External	**Opportunities** What strengths could you turn into opportunities? What is going on around you that you could capitalize on?	**Threats** What trends could be a risk or impediment to your plan? What weaknesses expose you? What obstacles do you foresee?

Once you are complete with the above SWOT you can work with your coach on taking it to the next level. For example, how you can use your strengths to address your opportunities etc.

If Not Now, When?

Many, if not most talented and ambitious Business Leaders consider going out on their own at one time or another. But few actually do it and that is why it's so important to discover what you value, your goals, transferable skills, and your risk tolerance. As a coach, I have helped motivate breakaway leaders to pause and build a strategy based on the requirements that fit them and their specific situation. If planned properly, whether they decide to remain as an employee or become a Business Owner, they benefit by thinking through their own change curve.

CHAPTER NINE
THE CHANGE CURVE

A few months ago, one of the members in my leadership program had to conduct his <u>sixth</u> layoff. He hired me to help him develop his leadership brand and prepare him to make the transition from a senior vice president to a C-level executive. I shared the below change curve with him to help him identify where he was within the change curve and to use it with his remaining team members. As he met with his team to discuss the upcoming changes, he noticed that some were scared, others were angry and a few were excited. As he thought about their range of emotions, he began to realize he needed his coach and Crew (our mastermind group) to help manage his own emotions.

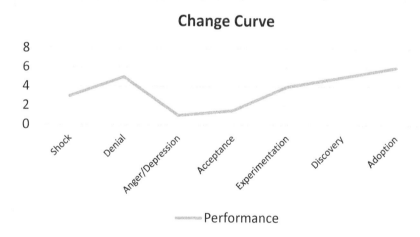

Change Curve

Performance

Change is a process and has various stages that both the individual and the organization will transition through. By understanding the emotions that are part of the stages, leaders can help themselves and others throughout the implementation of change. It is important as a leader that you model the behavior you want to see in others. Remember, if you don't take care of yourself first, you will not be able to effectively help the people around you whether at home or at work.

Stage 1: Shock. Employees are often shocked or surprised by change. They wonder, "Why?" and "What's going to happen?" Performance may initially decrease sharply; however, lack of productivity is usually brief. As a leader, be patient during this phase.

Stage 2: Denial. Many employees will enter into a phase of denial where they may minimize or deny that the change will occur. They think, "Oh, that won't affect me," or, "It will never happen." As a result, there is usually an increase in productivity to the level it was prior to the change trigger. In this phase it is important to stay consistent with the change message.

Stage 3: Anger and/or Depression. Employees begin to wonder what their role in the change will be, question their ability to make the necessary change, and may feel anxious about their future. Self-doubt is at the highest point and productivity decreases to an all-time low. Remember not to take any of this personally and if you're feeling this way remember no feeling lasts forever.

Stage 4: Acceptance. A more optimistic mood occurs when the employee acknowledges that the change is inevitable and decides to work with it. They understand the reason why the change is occurring and what their role is. Productivity begins to increase.

Stage 5: Experimentation. Employees begin testing new behaviors and skills required for the change. As employees test new behaviors they begin to discover which behaviors are effective and which are not. They begin to feel more hopeful and confident. Productivity is typically inconsistent as employees test and develop their new abilities. Some days we will be more productive and some days we won't because we are trying to figure out what works and what doesn't.

Stage 6: Discovery. The employees' process of identifying what works helps them to assign meaning to the new situation. The employees begin to understand why certain behaviors are effective while others are not. This understanding allows the employees to take more control over their actions and they become more strategic in their thinking and behavior. Confidence continues to grow and anxiety is replaced with excitement. Productivity increases.

Stage 7: Adoption. The final stage occurs when the employees have taken ownership of their new skills and behaviors. Confidence and competence increase and their new ways of doing business become natural. The old behaviors have been successfully replaced with new behaviors.

It is important to note that not all employees go through all of the stages of the Change Curve. Some will go from Stage Two to Stage Four. Others may remain in one stage longer than another.

The key is in understanding what stage your team is in and to validate their feelings as being part of the normal process of transition. Acknowledging your employees' emotions will also help you in determining how and when to communicate particular information, as well as gauging the amount of support they may need. It is also important, as leaders, to discuss your own feelings with trusted mentors and key members of your Crew. This leader continued to develop his Change Leadership capabilities as he was able to articulate his vision for the future, while being empathetic of others' emotions. We've had some great success with this tool; let us know how this works for you!

Scope the Change

Our organizations are constantly in a state of flux. If you've been working in corporate American long enough, I am sure you've had at least one of your leaders stand up and make an announcement similar to this, "There are going to be some changes around here..." Suddenly the room is buzzing as people start wondering what the change means and how it will affect them.

Change is inevitable, particularly in the workplace. While some individuals view it as frightening and stressful, others view it as exciting and motivating, a way to creatively move forward and enhance their goals and objectives. Rather than dreading change, learn to use it to your advantage. By understanding the process, you will not just get through it, you will be better because of it!

Most Common Types of Change:

1. **Developmental:** Simple and Predictable. Small incremental change. It does not change the core business strategy, e.g. releasing new software.

2. **Transitional:** Simple and Unpredictable or Complex & Predictable. Changes to structure, capabilities, and work processes (no changes to underlying business model/strategy), e.g. new organizational structure or reduction in staff.

3. **Transformational:** Complex and Unpredictable. Changes to completely redesign your business strategy and processes (implementing major strategic and cultural changes), e.g. core business model redesign and/or cultural norms.

Scoping the Change

Think back to an organizational change that did not occur. Now, based on your recollection, why do you suppose the change didn't happen? Is it possible that there weren't clear and consistent messages from key players in regards to exactly what was changing, why it was so important to change, your role in the change, and/or how you would know the change would result in an improvement? Yeah, I thought so.

Regardless of the type of change, leaders are usually clear on the business problem (a question, issue, or situation pertaining to the business that needs to be answered or resolved). However, oftentimes positive change doesn't occur because the change was not defined clearly by key players. When this occurs, it is easy for conflicting priorities or conflicting goals to negatively impact the strategy.

A while ago, I worked as an expert on a multi-year project with multiple work streams that impacted multiple people groups, processes and tools. Typically, in these large-scale projects, a change impact assessment is done at an enterprise level. More specifically, this means that the current- and future-state changes were documented across the enterprise, including management and customer-facing work processes and associated tools and technologies.

What is a Process?

A process is a group of activities that starts with an input and produces an output. A good process creates a valuable output (the customer determines if the process is valuable). When thinking about creating a change, it's important to know what processes will be impacted. Take a look at the Process Categories model which shows examples of various processes.

Process Categories

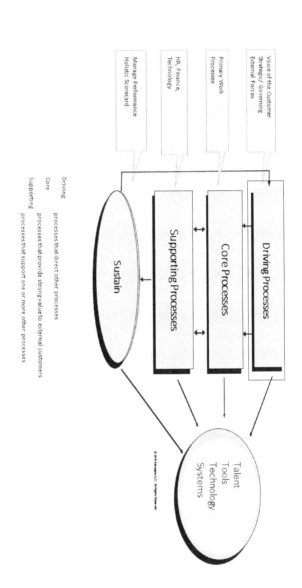

Voice of the Customer
Strategic/ Governing
External Forces

Primary Work
Processes

HR, Finance,
Technology

Manage Performance
Holistic Scorecard

Driving Processes

Core Processes

Supporting Processes

Sustain

Talent
Tools
Technology
Systems

Driving — processes that direct other processes

Core — processes that provide strong value to external customers

Supporting — processes that support one or more other processes

Change Definition Template

People and Knowledge

- Identify the Sponsors, Champions and Key Influencers for the change.

- Include what is expected of them and address concerns and any motivational or reward factors.

- This section may include beliefs, behaviors and assumptions for each people group.

- You may want to identify known communication and training activities here.

- Strong presence of sponsorship is needed.

- Support Key Influencers within the organization to become visibly engaged and communicate mutually agreed upon goals and successes.

Processes

- Review the process type section to assist with different types of processes that may be impacted.

- Driver, core and supporting processes must be aligned, monitored and enforced by Sponsor(s) and Key Influencers.

- Each process should be defined and aligned with Key Influencers.

Tools Technology & Methodology

- This section captures the Tools, Technology, and Methodologies surrounding the change.

- It assists leaders with addressing how the aforementioned plays a role within the current and desired state.

- Consistent use of Tools, Technologies and Methodologies will assist leaders with setting clear success measures and can support maintaining a viable reporting system for strategic decisions. In this way variability is lessened and synergy is built.

- Implement a holistic scorecard and dashboard for leaders to review and action key metrics that matter.

- Critical process measures should be actively addressed by Sponsors and Key Influencers via rewards & consequence measures.

Your Change Definition Template

People and Knowledge	
Processes	
Tools Technology & Methodology	

Change Case Study:

Kelly Smith, *Director of Sales*. Change occurring: Influx of new team members. The European employees must have stronger sales goal involvement and Kelly wants a greater span of control. She is focused on sales goals and she believes the more staff she has the greater likelihood of her success. She is afraid of appearing in a negative light among her peers. Ms. Smith does not listen to Jerry in operations because he constantly complains about being unprepared to deal with the additional process he needs to manage sales influx.

Kelly is afraid that she won't be able to get the necessary communications about process changes to him in time. We want her to feel confident that she will be involved in decisions that impact her position and will have the information she needs to give her peers. Currently she is aware of the change and is open to suggestion. However, she hasn't asked any additional questions to understand how this might impact her year-end leadership goals. We would like her to have stronger collaboration skills with her peers and influence with those that do not report to her directly. Once she is able to continue to negotiate and positively influence those around her, she will get a positive review and the team will celebrate with one day off.

Helpful Hints: Early change adopters and gatekeepers (anyone that oversees the change targets) should be involved from the onset in the shaping of the change. Be sure to include the change targets themselves. Further change management training by a good coach is an effective way to keep your most profitable changes in effect because it is not just about managing change, it is about ensuring integration and sustainability.

CHAPTER TEN
MAKE TIME FOR FUN!

Being in a transition can be challenging. So the intent of the following information is to support you with the clarity and confidence you need to be in the work-life of your dreams. It includes practical tools and ideas that we've gained over our years of experience.

TIME is our most valuable resource. We know there is always work to be done and that will NEVER change. The intention of this _section_ is to help you take back your time so that you can enjoy your best life now. We encourage you to daily check-in with yourself. We keep such a watchful eye on the future and our work goals that often we forget that life is a _journey_. If we are going to enjoy life and avoid professional burnout, we are going to have to learn to pause and live in the present moment.

10 Keys for Creating More Time and Less Stress

As busy professionals we seldom have big blocks of free time. Whether it's developing a new launch, managing day-to-day processes, or dealing with the necessary changes inside our organization, we tend to forget about ourselves or at least marginalize our personal needs, relegating them to the back of the to-do list. We neglect to remember that we are MORE than just Business Leaders. By carving out a moment (or moments) through the day for ourselves we will actually become BETTER in our profession! Here are some ways to get there.

1. _Remember to hit the PAUSE button_: During your workday you NEED to find moments to pause and catch your breath. Re-grounding yourself periodically throughout your day allows

you to be on top of your game and release the pressure that builds from constantly multi-tasking and making decisions.

If it is feasible, you might want to step outside for a few moments and breathe in the fresh air. Studies show NOTHING beats getting back to nature for reconnecting with our greater self. When this is not possible, an alternative resource that you can use right from your desk or mobile device is at www.calm.com. Download the app or use directly from your computer as a way to experience the rejuvenating effects of the outdoors. Take 5 minutes once an hour! (Carve out more if you can.)

2. **Create good centering habits:** Take time to read a positive affirmation, listen to a joke, or, heck, hum one of your favorite songs. Centering and refocusing ourselves on something positive boosts creativity and reduces feeling overwhelmed at the end of the day. Consider visiting Holstee.com to sign up for some great inspirational messages sent straight to your inbox.

3. **Find safety:** Talking to a trusted friend, mentor, mastermind group or coach for self-reflection can provide us with the clarity we need to handle any self-doubt or unnecessary self-criticism. We are harder on ourselves than ANYONE else! Confiding in safe people can help us to escape our own overly critical internal dialogue that can seem so hard to shut off at times.

4. **Plan for challenging interactions:** This may mean taking time to jot a few notes down before having a conversation with a challenging customer or co-worker. If we are not prepared for difficulties we know are coming, those interactions can increase our stress load or even throw a monkey wrench into our day. In the event that a challenging person catches you off guard, be sure to take a moment during the conversation to breathe in gentleness and breathe out calm. (Yes, it really does help!)

5. *Self-care*: Get an old-fashioned shave at a barber shop, go for a quick manicure, schedule a deep-tissue massage, or make that doctor's appointment you've been putting off. Make time to take care of yourself. Self-maintenance is an important part of staying physically, mentally and emotionally healthy. If you don't do it, who will?

6. *Learn to let the good in*: Take in that compliment! Don't discount it! If there is good coming your way let it in regardless of where it came from! You deserve good things! Sometimes it can be difficult to take positive affirmation from others. Don't deny yourself the pleasures of life!

7. *Get organized:* Make sure your work space is clean and well organized. If you haven't used something in a while, throw it away, give it away, or file it away from your workspace. By organizing our OUTSIDE environment, we are actually helping ourselves to organize our internal selves.

8. *Make a list:* Set your intentions for the day and list what you need to accomplish. Be sure to prioritize, separating urgent from non-urgent items, and you'll find it easier to accomplish them accordingly. Franklin Covey has created a great way to do this with his Time Matrix, part of a greater system that helps you to map out the most important tasks of your day.

9. *Cut out time killers*: You would be surprised by how much time you can save when you identify and cut out some of the biggest time killers in your workday. A great idea is to use an app like Rescue Time. It will help you audit your browsing time and highlight what is robbing you of your time during the day. (You will be astonished!)

   Another great idea is to "schedule" time to check your email rather than just responding every time your inbox or assistant's chimes. Email is a great tool but sometimes it can be distracting and counter-productive when it interrupts you every time you are making headway on a more pressing task. Perhaps you can plan to check your inbox during the morning, right after lunch, and close enough to the end of your day to sort and prioritize replies for the next workday.

10. *Live in the now:* Remind yourself of what is important right now (insert current day and time here), not yesterday and not tomorrow. Try focusing on one item at a time. Living in the present moment is the key to everything else listed above. We learn from the past. We aim for the future. But when it really comes down to it, ALL we ever have is this moment right now. Live IN it. Enjoy it. Appreciate it.

The 10 Keys above are a great way for you to create more time for yourself and decrease your daily stress. Sounds great in theory, right? What about those Last-minute requests that always seem to popup and try and rob you of the all-important "you" time that you are so desperate to keep?

Check out the next section for tips on how to protect yourself and manage those situations that will inevitably come up.

Secrets to Handling Last-Minute Requests, Like You Knew They Were Coming

I have held many roles throughout my career. I have been both the top dog leading others, as well as the one having to report to the "boss," so I know first-hand how to respond to last-minute requests. (Unfortunately for others I work with, I also know how to create unexpected requests!) I am pleased to provide you with the exercise below to help you **"Handle last-minute requests like you knew they were coming."**

Imagine the following situation: *It's one hour before you're ready to leave and everything is flowing as it should. You're on time with specific tasks and set to be done by the end of the day. Suddenly, a message appears in your inbox and it's from one of your top Clients. It is one of her quick, turn-around assignments and she wants it done before you leave for the day. To get it completed on time, you would have to drop everything and scramble to make it happen.*

Fighting back the urge to blurt out, **"I'm not a miracle worker!"** you realize that the aggravation is only taking up time and energy that you could be using to complete the given task. This used to drive me nuts!

Give the short action plan below a try the next time you are under the gun:

Remember, this is not a personal attack: We naturally rise to a challenge; it's our survival instinct, but remember that having insufficient time to complete a last-minute request is not a reflection of you personally. In fact, your Client may not even be aware that the request is unreasonable. Just don't waste time dwelling on the negative. You're a professional!

Don't be afraid to ask for clarification: If you feel as though the quality of the assignment will be greatly impacted by the time constraint, clarify with your Client if the last-minute request is a _want_ or a _need_. If it is a need, drop the perfectionism and do exactly what your Client is asking—with no bells and no whistles. Dig in and do your best with the time you've been given.

Act decisively: Your role is to quickly evaluate or clarify the nature of the request and then act accordingly. Figure out if there is actually enough time left to complete the new task. Could your current task be delayed until the next day? Is the new assignment "now or never," or does it just feel like it?

Have Clear Boundaries & Limitations: Remember the "carrying more than your own weight" concept I mentioned? We're all guilty of it and it often causes a complexity in the prioritizing department. A productive leader knows their limits and works within those parameters. If you push your limits too far, your health, the quality of your delivery, and your productivity go down. A good Client will not want you to suffer for a piece of paper. Remember, in order to be the best possible resource for your Client, they (s/he) need to understand when you are reaching full capacity.

Ask yourself if this is a regular occurrence. If this is a regular occurrence it may be best to schedule time to address the issue directly with your Client. Speak calmly using I statements and suggest a solution. Oftentimes, check-point meetings help align expectations and avoid last-minute requests. If this is not a regular occurrence, and you are confident that a few extra minutes will get the job done then use your best judgment and move ahead with it.

Be honest. Be practical, but DON'T underestimate yourself! There is a fine line between telling ourselves "I can't," and a dismissive, "I just really don't want to." Set realistic expectations for the request but still give it your all! Give these techniques a try the next time you are squeezed to make something out of nothing.

Stress Management Action Plan

Identify three main areas in which you want to manage stress better. Include what you will do when you are stressed AND how you will act when you do not handle stress well.

Stress Triggers	Leadership SuperPower in Action
1.	1.
2.	2.
3.	3.

How will you measure your success?

1.

2.

3.

How will you be with yourself when you don't handle your stress well, e.g. self-compassion? Revisit this section of the book to better balance your work and personal life. Make sure you are following many of the above techniques to reduce your stress load and find "Time for Fun"!

CHAPTER ELEVEN
CALL TO ACTION!
YES, YOUR ACTION!

We are living in rapidly changing times and the paradigms of the past are undergoing an evolution. At the same time, the meaning of work-life balance is making many people re-evaluate what their priorities are now and for the future. Technology, globalization, and a nebulous international financial system are sending signals for many to seriously consider their options. There are many exciting options and none without some risk. The beauty is, there are strategies to prepare and plan for success and a ton of expertise out there now available 24/7, any place in the world. The vast experiences, skills and talents of others are now accessible to you like never before.

Since most of us have become specialists, our working world has become overly focused and has left most professionals vulnerable to the sweeping changes that seem headed our way. As a result, many feel the need to analyze their options and future career paths and do some proactive planning. That very new market is the jurisdiction of the professional coach.

No matter how smart or talented a person is, the evolving markets and workplace rules and data are just too much for one person to know or understand. But the internet and the digital marketplace have made it possible for anybody to acquire knowledge of just about any kind. The questions for you are about *when* and *how* to get started. To whom do you turn for advice and guidance on something you may not be familiar enough with to even ask the right questions? **What if there was one place you could go to build your leadership legacy?**

Like I've said, over the years, I've spent so much money to learn how to grow a business with the highest level of integrity while leveraging the most innovative business techniques. Although I don't regret my investments, I wish there had been one place where I could go for help, instead of the multiple experiences I had to go through in order to know exactly what I needed to do.

As the demands of the workplace are changing, so too are the dreams and aspirations that many have formulated based on what was known of the past and what the imagined future holds. There is an instinctive feeling that some fundamental changes in economics will change the way Americans live in the future. This perception suggests that if we may be running out of what made us fulfilled in the past (mostly consumption of goods and services), it is logical to change what makes a person happy; something we can control **if properly defined**.

It bears repeating that, although I am known as a practical transformation expert, I recognize that I can't create Transformation on my own. Part of my journey has always involved putting the right people around me to support my continuous growth and development. There is a magic in participating in a leadership program and mastermind groups that no one can describe. My approach to helping you succeed is about combining an individual coaching experience, and business and leadership tools, along with the support of a mastermind network.

Any good professional coach can help you with the technical skills of a business, and help you define what makes you feel happy and fulfilled. Economics, lifestyle and the desire to be productive are key ingredients in accomplishing the ability to have choices, but therein lies the challenge. It requires planning with a high degree of real-world input and not just supposition. Being in a relationship with a good coach and mastermind group can help thinking people pull together the best information to help them make decisions based on their real life discoveries. If those personal factors are identified along with an action plan, the fear of change can be pushed way down the list of distractions that assault us every day.

Armed with knowledge and understanding of what you really want can clear the path for your fulfillment and financial success. If you or anybody you know is anxious about their future work-life balance, it's a good first step to contact a professional coach. They are much more than just business consultants because they are focused not only on the business but also on you as a person.

In closing, I'd like to say, if you want every day to be like a Friday, you need to be Aligned, have a great Crew, make a commitment to your Transformation Strategy and know your Transition Plan. Some people make excuses and tell themselves, "I don't have time for this Alignment work." The truth is, we all have the same amount of time. In this case, it is really a matter of our priorities, not a matter of time.

Listen, I get it; change is scary. Investing in ourselves is also new for some of us but please, don't just get by as best you can without utilizing these tools designed to benefit you. I stand for you, your Leader Within and your work in this world. **The bottom line is that living your life fully is much easier when you surround yourself with a Crew that has tools and is committed to walk alongside you as you Transform.** Don't be afraid to reach out and let people see who you really are. As my friend Meg always reminds me, "Assume people will like you." Join that leadership program or mastermind group, get the mentor or coach you respect. They need you too, you know. Commit to having time and space in your life for Transformation to occur.

It's great to dream, and it's even better when you have a plan! You can't have a plan without knowing your end game (your Transition Plan). The truth is that no matter what we do on the outside, no matter how much money we make or don't make, what relationship we have, when we feel successful we are fulfilled. Most people live their lives on Ready, Set then Go. But when you're making EVERY day Friday, I invite YOU to appropriately let your inner teenager out to say **"Go, Set, Ready." Your Leader Within will help you, Align yourself, get a good Crew, commit to your Transformation Strategy and get a good Transition Plan.**

Additional Stories about Real Leaders

Finally, I'd like to share a few stories about my clients. Below is a note that I received a short while ago from one of my clients who is the SVP of Corporate Development within his company. "Hello Nina, I need your help. I seem to have a growing problem with my sales director and technology director. They don't seem to like each other very much. My sales director has been complaining that he isn't getting his reports normally provided by the IT department.

When I asked our IT director about it, she became upset and mentioned that she thought the sales director was acting like her boss and trying to manipulate her department to prioritize his needs over the needs of others.

Here is my dilemma: I need them to get along. How do I get them to take action without either of them feeling like I am taking sides?" My answer: The first order of business is to create alignment. In this case, it starts with you (SVP of Corporate Development) understanding what you're doing to create a good environment for your directors to get along. Second, create a common goal of having each director recognize that they are customers of one another.

After my client and I spoke, he asked each of his directors to answer the following question of one another, "How might we work together in order that we both get our needs met?" *After a few sessions together, we discovered that they not only had different work preferences, their processes and success measures were not aligned.*

Here is another story about a Business Leader transitioning back into the world of entrepreneurship. I was in-between client sessions, and my phone rang. One of my leadership program members called, and I could immediately hear the excitement in his voice.

For the past few months, I had been working closely with him to make his dream of being a full-time entrepreneur take shape. **He Aligned his values with the work he wanted to do. Then he engaged his Crew (his mastermind group in our leadership program) to help him ensure his business offerings were valuable based on the needs of his customers. He committed to making time for his own Transformation** with his Coach (me) and he developed his Leadership Stake for his business. After that he created a plan to <u>T</u>ransition from his current position including the necessary financials. He was calling me to let me know that he was ready to take the leap forward and his transition was happening that week!!!

From his first words, I knew immediately how much this meant to him. He was achieving his higher professional purpose of creating more authentic business model that aligned with his legacy as a leader. At the same time, he was gaining the personal flexibility he craved for his family and home life. This was no longer a dream for him; it was real and he was actively creating the future we had worked together to achieve.

Now many people do not need to leave their current employer to be fulfilled so listen to my next story.

One of my leadership program clients who had been with a good company for a long while, AND he was underpaid in relationship with the market for his position. So he called me and wondered how he could apply for another position that was potentially out of reach.

As we reviewed his **ACTT Blueprint** including his values assessment and his transferable skills, we created an amazing resume and cover letter for him to submit for the position. As we waited for a rejection letter or an interview, we conducted a few mock C-Suite interviews ourselves and he realized that he had the leadership skills AND the talent to go rock the new position.

When he got the call for the interview, the Crew in his mastermind group cheered and continued to support him with what they saw as his strengths as a leader. In our next mastermind session, he announced that he got the call and actually landed the new Director position (at 34 years of age!) with a Fortune 500 company, and with an 80% salary increase! We had an amazing moment of inspiration and celebration! I am not going to lie to you; he worked hard to get where he is today. Maybe you won't get an 80% increase by going for a position you really want, but the question for you is: wouldn't it be worth a try?

I simply can't tell you the excitement that the entire mastermind group still has about him landing such a great position without an endless parade of ever-more complicated (ever-more exhausting) tools and tactics. Creating financial freedom takes energy, focus and commitment, AND you don't have to drive yourself crazy to do it.

Now maybe you are hesitating. You don't really think things are that bad. In fact, you might think things could be better if you just left things alone. Here is a story about one of my leadership program participants, in his words. "I didn't think that I needed help, but of course I did—on numerous fronts."

"On the personal side, I discovered that I was close to living my dream: spending significant time with family and not worrying about money. However, I needed to secure this by actually having money, so it was important to align my personal future with my career future. My future career wishes were, typically for me, pragmatic. However, I didn't have a plan to *get* there. They were a dream for the future, and I needed to get started. Sometimes all that was needed was a gentle prodding, and other times I got the (completely necessary) verbal kicking I needed. The program is tuned for your needs: along with timely and topical one-on-one discussions, they skilfully use the right tools from their toolbox, at the right time."

"Guys don't make close friends quickly—we make acquaintances quickly, and friends in due course. However, the program once again broke down barriers. Each of us was going through our own version of The Lone Ranger: struggling to do the right thing for ourselves and our families. Many of us felt unworthy to be in the group, but we were well matched. As we were learning about ourselves we met as a group, and became closer through this shared experience. The program is finished for me, but I know that I can call upon them if I have a need. I will support them in any way I can. After all, they're my friends."

Another story is from one of my leadership program clients, an SVP in Technologies. He has been working with us to develop his Visionary SuperPower in order to reach his development goal of being a CIO (Chief Information Officer). This is his feedback to us (his Crew) after our first face-to-face mastermind session.

"I really, really, really (did I say really?) liked yesterday. I found all of it valuable; however, I found the challenge of the goal setting and being personally challenged to evolve the best. One lasting image for me was your comment on 'being upset that I was too humble' and Shani's reinforcement that I need to **do more with my vision***. Loved it. Without being stretched and challenged, the muscles won't grow...Just continue to push and force me to dig deeper.* This is one of the best learning experiences I've ever had. **Continue to provide feedback around how others see my brand, so I can continue this journey of change....** "

With all of our apps and technology, we have a false sense of independence, and although we don't "need" one another for our basic survival, we could all use a little smooth-sailing in our lives. Towards that end, my client has taken the past six months to develop a strong professional Crew. Why? Well, he could instead just float on his natural abilities, yet he decided to listen to his Leader Within and develop himself even further.

Now maybe some of you know you want a business of your own but you just hate sales and marketing and based on the crazy developments I see out there, I completely get it. Here is another story about one of my leadership program clients in your shoes. She is truly one of the most natural, transformational coaches I've ever had the pleasure of being around! Although she wanted to launch her own business, she hates marketing and sales! It's been a few months since we started to work together.

Here is what she has to say about our program, "As for marketing, one day on a call and you said to me, "We need to find a business plan that flows for you. It will be different than mine." That made me feel really seen and heard. Further the biggest revelation for me has been CREW. I've seen it shift from a concept to truly coming to life. Before we started working together, I had zero professional crew members. Now my crew is robust and growing-- feeding each other's progress and finding new ways to plug in my gifts."

Why does she feel so fulfilled? Because she has the right business model, designed specifically for her. She has a Relational SuperPower—a true people person. So her "sales" model is more about connection, crew and relationship rather than writing blogs every day. Conversely, my model is based on creation! **Which business model is right for you?**

This is my final story, and one of my favorites. A few months ago, I got a call from one of my inner-circle members. He sounded conflicted. Although he had just sold his program to a corporate client, he didn't know how he was going to tell his wife that he was ready to quit his job and take the jump into fulltime self-employment.

We reviewed his **ACTT** tools including his "leadership stake" for his business. Then we talked about how he could further engage his Crew within and outside our leadership program. As he processed his financial forecast, his Transformation Strategy and his Transition Plan, he focused on his priorities and, albeit nervously, was ready to have this life-changing conversation with his wife later that evening.

The next day, I called to check in with him. When he answered the phone, I found myself caught up in his story of how his wife had full confidence in him and although she was used to a consistent income, she would rather take the risk with him than have him just survive at his job. My eyes teared as I realized that he had found a much higher sense of prosperity. Then I headed off to enjoy my day, with the warm feeling of having made a difference for someone. I realize it's easy to get caught up in our day to day world, but here's the deal, think about how others might benefit from YOU Living like Every Day is Friday, and let that motivate you to keep moving forward.

Let's make this real for you:

- How important is a life well-lived to you?

- What is your legacy as a leader?

- How aligned are your personal values with the work you actually do? (e.g. self-care is my highest priority value yet sometimes I work more than I should.) How about you?

- What will you do to create a more positive work environment for you and those around you?

- How do you describe the value you offer to others in your work-life?

- If I asked five other people you work with to describe the value you provide, how closely will it Align with what you just said?

In the beginning of the book, I asked you to remember how you felt. Assuming you read everything and completed all the exercises, how do you feel now? Inspired and informed I hope! Thank you for letting me be a part of making every day Friday for YOU!

For further information about how we can help inspire your leadership legacy, please contact Metaspire LLC, c/o Nina Segura, 7100 WEST CAMINO REAL, SUITE 302 BOCA RATON, FLORIDA 33433 PHONE: 1 (877) 786-9995 or Visit www.NinaSegura.com

ABOUT THE AUTHOR

Raised by a single Mom in Davie, Florida, Nina grew up with little means. Initially a Crew of one, she began working at an early age to create the business and life she wanted. Nina was driving at four-teen, and by the age of sixteen, she plunged her Chevelle SS into a canal, learning what would be the first in a series of valuable lessons.

At 17 years old, Nina joined Amex where she ascended the corporate ladder, and received numerous awards for quality by saving millions of dollars in global multi-year projects. Nina graduated with Honors from NOVA Southeastern University, receiving a Bachelor of Science degree in Professional Management, and has also attained a Master's in Organization Management from the University of Phoenix. She studied with Peter Senge and was an Advisor to his Society of Learning in North America. Nina is a Certified Professional Co-Active Coach, Project Manager and Certified Six Sigma Blackbelt, and also an International Coach Federation Mentor. She is also a CTI and MIT - SOL-NA Leadership Graduate.

In 2005, as an Amex Global Project Manager, Nina decided to leave Amex and start Metaspire Consulting. Nina took Metaspire from start-up to millions of dollars in sales in just five years. In response to her client's needs, she created BusinessCoachingOnDemand.com and SuperVirtualTeams.com. Nina's specialty is inspiring your legacy as a leader.

For over 20 years, Nina Segura has delivered insight and mo-tivation for Business Owners and corporate leaders within companies such as Carnival Cruise Lines, American Express, BCBS and many more. She is a fierce leader that gets those around her to take notice. There is no hiding in the back of the room when Nina is around. She calls forth each and every leader to examine the truths in their business and life actions. Then Nina wakes them up by having you commit to taking at least one positive action step that day; Making Every Day Friday!

Nina Segura MA, CSSBB, CPCC's work has appeared in Amex Open Forum, iHeartRadio and iTunes. Her experiential approach inspires others to take at least one positive action step that day.

Every Day is Friday!!! is filled with inspiring stories of real-life leaders who are committed to making a positive impact in our world. It is for those in the business world who are trying to make sense of what is happening to them during their mid-life. *Every Day is Friday!!!* provides practical business tools and powerful questions for the mindset necessary to move beyond the challenges of change that inevitably come our way.

Nina's keynote speech, "How to Make Every Day Friday" is a highly interactive program for Business Leaders, and entrepreneurs. She shares decades of research revealing proven secrets to a lasting leadership legacy. You will learn the exact framework for having every day look and feel like Friday faster and easier than ever before.

ACKNOWLEDGEMENTS

To my husband and romantic life partner, Jeff. You are a leader of leaders. Your focus and tenacity is incomparable. I would not be where I am today if it wasn't for you. I love to laugh with you; to stand by your side and share life's experiences with you.

To my sister Babs who is a model of living her values, especially life-long learning and self-care!

To Gini Rinkus my number one fan and the first person to purchase this book (prior to the book being written).

To Penn Moody who had no idea that being a lifelong learner coupled with his commitment to leaving a positive legacy on this earth would fuel the backbone of this book.

Thank you, Mary C. Owens, MSW, CTACC, Transitional Expert, for supporting me with your knowledge in the Change Curve section.

To The Coaches Training Institute founders Karen and Henry Kimsey-House, without your stand to see the good in everyone and your willingness to cultivate positive leadership in our world, this work would have not been possible for me.

To Rick Tamlyn and Helen House, my leaders, because you choose to do your own deep work, you make our world a better place. I will never forget hearing Rick telling me to Recover, nor Helen calling me on my Assumptions. Just AwesomeSauce!!!

APPENDIX A
SELECT CLIENT TESTIMONIALS

Please note that I have changed some names to uphold Client Relationships.

"As a business leader, I always have Nina at the top of my mind, when I need clarity and alignment, helping me to become a better leader and build my own dream team. I have recently participated in her mastermind program, and could not be more satisfied with the results I obtained." **— American Express Business Travel**

"Nina is one of the best consultants I have worked with. She is highly analytical and able to recommend a path to success even in a very difficult situation. Nina showed me and my organization a way to multiply the bottom line in a highly effective way. I was amazed by Nina's professional attitude and how fast she could undertake and deliver a very detailed analysis and present it in a very insightful way." **— Dolby Laboratories**

"Nina Segura is a very talented coach! She has an in-depth knowledge of the techniques of Co-Active Coaching plus an intuitive ability to home in on what is really going on. She is awesome and amazing. And lots of fun to be around!" **— NASA**

"Nina tailors her methodologies in exceptional and unique ways to bring value to her clients and their staff. I was very fortunate to have

worked with Nina and highly recommend her in every way."
— Tenet Healthcare

"I highly recommend Nina. She has proven to be an engaged and passionate member of any organization she supports. I met Nina while working as a Director of Business Process Improvement at American Express. She immediately showed her passion for Organizational Design work and became the change management leader on the team. Nina supported me in several key areas, including organizational development support for an extensive CMMI benchmarking project that identified over $200 million in savings by restructuring software development processes." **— AET Global Reengineering**

"I have worked with Nina for over two years...She constantly pushes the envelope, always trying another way until success is attained. She is creative and innovative in her idea generation and applies critical and strategic thinking to all situations. She is not only an advocate of the five disciplines of organizational learning, but has astute competencies from a systems perspective in each (systems thinking, shared vision, team learning, mental models and personal mastery). Great team player and fun to work with—a real energizer bunny!" **—Council Member at Society for Organizational Learning North America**

"I was impressed that Nina took full responsibility, not as a contractor or temporary help. They put in time and effort above what was expected of a coach or trainer, staying late or starting meeting early, if necessary. They made the relationship easy by developing a good rapport with both the client and employees." **— Kaplan, Inc.**

"Nina facilitated process modeling workshops for the development of Hewlett Packard's Global Marketing Enterprise Architecture. Through these workshops HP realized a conservative $67 Million saved

in operating expenses within the first year."— **Hewlett Packard Global Marketing Operations**

"While with American Express, received the Chairman's Premier Tier 1 Award for mapping the technical requirements for the Dispute Handling System. The net effect of Nina and her team's efforts resulted in an estimated savings of $10M dollars per year."—**Global SN American Express**

"Nina is one of a kind. I worked with Nina at American Express and have stayed in contact with her ever since. She is extremely professional, yet touches you on a personal level with her understanding and caring for you as a professional. Your success is her goal, and she is one of the best I have met at making sure what you want to achieve is successful."— **Global Technology Delivery, Merrill Corporation**

"Nina Segura is an engaging and energetic speaker. Her passion and presence breathe life into her message, captivating her audience and creating an atmosphere of receptivity."— **People of Diversity**

"Everyone was engaged. No one was looking at their phones! One of the participants came to us afterwards and said they applied the leadership model to respond to a retort from their director and it brought them together!"— **Carnival Cruise Lines**

APPENDIX B
BIBLIOGRAPHY OF RECOMMENDED READING

Below are a few Leadership, Team and Business books I recommend:

7 Habits of Highly Effective People—Stephen Covey

Blink: The Power of Thinking Without Thinking—Malcolm Gladwell

Co-Active Leadership: Five Ways to Lead—Henry Kimsey-House and Karen Kimsey-House

The Stake – Henry Kimsey-House

Creating Leaderful Organizations: How to Bring out Leadership in Everyone—Berret-Koehler Publishers

Delivering Happiness—Tony Hsieh

First Break All the Rules—Curt Coffman and Marcus Buckingham

Good to Great, Why Some Companies Make the Leap and Others Don't—Jim Collins

How to Analyze the Small and Medium-Size Enterprise—Len Goodman

How to Win Friends and Influence People—Dale Carnegie

Leadership and Self Deception—Getting out of the Box—Arbinger Institute

Leadership from the Inside Out—Kevin Cashman

Overcoming the Five Dysfunctions of a Team: A Field Guide for Leaders, Managers, and Facilitators—Patrick Lencioni

Overwhelmed: Work, Love and Play When No One Has the Time—Bridgid Schulte

Presence: Human Purpose and the Field of the Future—Senge et al.

Primal Leadership: Realizing the Power of Emotional Intelligence—Margaret Wheatley

Profit from The Positive—Margaret Greenbery & Senia Maymin

Reinventing Organizations—Frederic Laloux

Rich Dad, Poor Dad—Robert T. Kiyosaki

Before you Quit Your Job—Robert T. Kiyosaki with Sharon L. Lechter, C.P.A.

Start with Why—Simon Sinek

The Fifth Discipline Field Book—Peter Senge, et al.

The Four Agreements: A Practical Guide to Personal Freedom—Don Miguel Ruiz

The OZ Principle—Craig Hickman

The Power of Full Engagement—Jim Loehr

The Power of No—James & Claudia Altucher

The Sacred Six: The Simple Step-by-Step Process for Focusing Your Attention—JB Glossinger

The NEW Stress Response Diet and Lifestyle Program—Bill Cortright

Think and Grow Rich—Napoleon Hill

Tribal Leadership—David Logan, et al.

Tribes: We Need You to Lead Us—Seth Godin

Turning to One Another: Simple Conversations to Restore Hope to the Future—Margaret Wheatley

CPSIA information can be obtained
at www.ICGtesting.com
Printed in the USA
BVHW04s2052041018
529213BV00025B/93/P